BOOKBINDER'S

Tony's

Biggs

Le Cordon Bleu

Blue Fox

Le Ruth's

Pontchartrain Wine Cellars

THE "21" CLUB

Charlie's café exceptionale

charley's crab

Danny's

MISTER A.

BENSON & HEDGES 100's,
in its continuing series of volumes
dedicated to good taste,
invites you to savor the elegance
and excitement of America's
finest cuisine in this collection of

**100 RECIPES
FROM 100 OF THE
GREATEST RESTAURANTS**

Recipes selected and edited by Pat Jester
Photography by William K. Sladcik
Food styling by Fran Paulson
Produced by Meredith Publishing Services

Cover Recipes:

Coq Sauté au Riesling d'Alsace from Lutèce,
New York City (page 64)

The Old Warsaw Salad from La Vieille Varsovie,
Dallas, Texas (page 98)

Praline Ice Cream Pie from Fournou's Ovens,
San Francisco (page 113)

The food photography in this book is designed
to provide ideas for serving the recipes in your
home and does not necessarily represent the
way the dishes are served in the various
restaurants.

Published by
Philip Morris Incorporated
for Benson & Hedges 100's
100 Park Avenue
New York, New York 10017

Printed in the United States of America

FOREWORD

The idea for this book came up several years ago. We'd just put to press the first Benson & Hedges 100's book of "100 of the World's Greatest Recipes" with the help of our good friend Craig Claiborne. As we looked ahead, we thought about doing a book of recipes from America's great restaurants. Then we had the good fortune to work with James Beard, and his volume became last year's contribution to good dining from Benson & Hedges 100's.

This year we decided the dream could wait no longer. We developed a plan, selected 100 of the greatest restaurants in America with the same care you might use in choosing one for an evening out, asked for their recipes and tested each one.

The result is this unique collection! There really is no other like it. It shares with you what 100 great chefs have shared with us — the ingredients, the secrets, the subtleties that are the great cuisine of America.

So, turn the pages and enjoy. Discover how to prepare Bananas Foster the way they do at Brennan's in New Orleans; grace your table with Vitello Tartufatto in the style of La Scala of Beverly Hills; awaken your appetite with Cafe Johnell's Truite Soufflé. And this is just the beginning — there are 97 more recipes to choose from.

Benson & Hedges 100's welcomes you to the company of America's great chefs.

Bon appetit!

CONTENTS

Crêpe St. Jacques

½ cup all-purpose flour
½ cup milk
2 egg yolks
 Dash salt

. . .

¼ cup finely chopped green onion
1 cup chopped fresh mushrooms
2 tablespoons butter
¼ cup dry white wine
1 tablespoon all-purpose flour
1 cup light cream
 Dash salt

. . .

1 tablespoon butter
4 ounces shrimp, cooked, cleaned, and cut up

. . .

2 egg yolks
4 teaspoons lemon juice
½ teaspoon prepared mustard
 Dash cayenne
6 tablespoons butter

. . .

2 tablespoons sliced almonds

Crêpes: In bowl, combine flour, milk, 2 egg yolks, and dash salt. Beat smooth with rotary beater. Using 1 scant tablespoon batter for each crêpe, prepare crêpes by spooning batter into a hot lightly greased skillet or griddle and spreading with back of spoon into a 3-inch circle. Brown on one side only; remove to paper toweling. Makes 12 crêpes.

Wine Sauce: Cook green onion and ½ cup of the mushrooms in 2 tablespoons butter till tender. Add white wine. Simmer, reducing liquid by half. Blend 1 tablespoon all-purpose flour, light cream, and dash salt; add all at once to onion mixture. Cook and stir till mixture bubbles.

Filling: In skillet, melt 1 tablespoon butter. Cook remaining ½ cup of the mushrooms in butter till tender. Stir in shrimp. Remove from heat; stir in 2 tablespoons of the wine sauce. Place 1 tablespoon filling on unbrowned side of each crêpe. Roll up. Place seam side down in 10x6x2-inch baking dish. Pour remaining mushroom-wine sauce over crêpes; cover and bake in 375° oven for 20 minutes. Uncover. Spoon some Hollandaise Sauce over each crêpe. Sprinkle with almonds. Broil 3 inches from heat for 2 to 3 minutes till browned. Makes 12 appetizers.

Blender Hollandaise: Put 2 egg yolks, lemon juice, prepared mustard, and cayenne in blender container; blend till ingredients are combined. Heat 6 tablespoons butter in saucepan till melted and almost boiling. With blender slowly running, slowly pour about a third of the hot butter, in a thin stream, into blender container. Turn blender to high speed; slowly pour in remaining hot butter, blending till mixture is smooth and thickened.

Carmel-by-the-Sea, California

Escargots à la Marquis

   2 cups mushrooms, sliced
   2 tablespoons chopped shallots
   2 4½-ounce cans snails, drained (36 snails)
¼ cup butter
½ cup light cream
½ teaspoon dried thyme, crushed
   1 small bay leaf, crumbled
½ teaspoon salt
⅛ teaspoon pepper
½ cup Madeira wine

In saucepan, cook mushrooms, shallots, and

snails in butter till mushrooms are tender. Stir in cream, thyme, bay leaf, salt, and pepper; simmer, uncovered, 10 minutes. Add Madeira; heat through. Serve in individual casseroles. Makes 6 to 8 servings.

Masson's

New Orleans, Louisiana

Oysters Beach House

- ¼ cup sliced mushrooms
- 2 tablespoons chopped shallots or green onion
- 1½ teaspoons dry mustard
  Dash cayenne
- 3 tablespoons butter
- 3 tablespoons all-purpose flour
- ½ teaspoon salt
- ¾ cup milk
- 1 beaten egg yolk
- 2 tablespoons dry sherry
- 12 small oysters
  Salt

In saucepan, cook mushrooms, shallots, mustard, and cayenne in butter till vegetables are tender but not brown. Blend in flour and ½ teaspoon salt. Add milk. Cook and stir till thickened and bubbly. Gradually add the sauce to egg yolk; return to saucepan. Cook 1 minute more. Stir in sherry.

Place raw oysters in shells in shallow baking pan; sprinkle with salt. Bake in 350° oven for 8 minutes, till nearly done. Spoon some sauce over each oyster (about 1 tablespoon each). Bake 5 minutes longer. Makes 12 appetizers.

Cold Salmon "21" with Pressed Cucumbers and Sauce Verte

    1 3½- to 4-pound dressed salmon,
         head and tail removed
    1 cup dry white wine
   ½ cup white vinegar
    3 cups water
    1 small onion, chopped (¼ cup)
    1 stalk celery, chopped (½ cup)
    1 teaspoon salt
   ¼ teaspoon leaf thyme, crushed
    1 bay leaf
         Thin lemon and lime slices
    1 envelope unflavored gelatin

         .   .   .

    2 medium cucumbers
         Salt
    1 tablespoon mayonnaise
  1½ teaspoons lemon juice
   ¼ teaspoon ground nutmeg
   ⅛ teaspoon pepper

         .   .   .

   ½ cup torn spinach
   ¼ cup chopped watercress
   ¼ cup chopped parsley
   ¼ cup sliced leeks
  1½ teaspoons snipped chives
    1 cup mayonnaise

Place fish on greased rack in fish poacher. Add wine, vinegar, water, onion, celery, salt, thyme, and bay leaf. Bring to boil; reduce heat. Cover and poach 20 to 25 minutes, or till fish flakes easily when tested with a fork. Remove from heat; allow salmon to cool slightly in poaching liquid (15 to 20 minutes).

Remove salmon from poacher, reserving liquid. Carefully remove skin with sharp knife. Transfer fish to large serving platter. Garnish with overlapping row of lemon and lime slices (or other garnishes). Cover and chill fish about 1 hour.

Meanwhile, strain broth through several thicknesses of cheesecloth, reserving 2 cups. In small saucepan, sprinkle gelatin over the 2 cups of cooled broth; let stand 5 minutes till softened. Heat and stir over low heat till gelatin is dissolved. Chill till partially set.

Quickly spoon some gelatin glaze over fish and fruit slices; chill fish. Keep remaining glaze at room temperature. (If glaze becomes too thick, reheat, then chill till partially set.) Spoon remaining glaze over fish. Chill thoroughly. Before serving, remove any glaze from platter. Serve with Pressed Cucumbers and Sauce Verte. Makes 6 to 8 servings.

Pressed Cucumbers: Peel and halve cucumbers lengthwise; remove seeds. Slice very thinly (4 cups). Place in sieve over bowl; sprinkle generously with salt. Place a heavy weight atop cucumbers. Let stand 1 to 2 hours to drain thoroughly. To serve, combine cucumbers, the 1 tablespoon mayonnaise, the lemon juice, nutmeg, and pepper; chill, if desired. Makes 2¾ cups.

Sauce Verte: In small saucepan, cook spinach, watercress, parsley, leeks, and chives, covered in ¼ cup boiling, lightly salted water for 5 minutes. Drain well; cool. In blender container combine cooked vegetables and the 1 cup mayonnaise. Cover and blend smooth. Chill. Makes 1¼ cups.

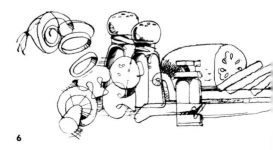

PIER 66

Crab Fritters with Rebel Sauce

¼ cup chopped shallots
 2 tablespoons butter
½ cup white wine
½ cup finely diced green pepper
¼ cup diced pimiento
 1 tablespoon chopped parsley
⅛ teaspoon salt
    Dash bottled hot pepper sauce
    Dash cayenne
 1 6-ounce package frozen king crab meat,
    thawed and coarsely chopped (1¼ cups)
 3 cups soft white bread crumbs (4 slices)
 3 beaten egg yolks
    Oil for deep frying

    . . .

½ cup orange marmalade
 2 tablespoons orange juice
 1 tablespoon lemon juice
1½ teaspoons prepared horseradish
⅛ teaspoon ground ginger
¼ teaspoon dry mustard

In 10-inch skillet, cook shallots in butter for 2 to 3 minutes. Add wine. Boil until liquid is almost all evaporated. Meanwhile, add green pepper to a small pan of boiling water. Cook 30 seconds; drain. Add to skillet along with pimiento, parsley, salt, hot pepper sauce, and cayenne. Add crab and bread crumbs. Toss lightly. Add egg yolks; mix till blended.

Using about 2 tablespoons of mixture, shape into "silver dollar" pancakes. Fry in deep oil (365°) about 1 to 1½ minutes or till browned. Serve 3 or 4 per person with Rebel Sauce.

Rebel Sauce: In blender container, combine remaining ingredients. Blend just till combined. Heat in small saucepan. Makes ¾ cup.

Paglia e Fieno
(Straw and Hay)

- 3 ounces green noodles
- 3 ounces white noodles
- 1 cup whipping cream
- 2 tablespoons butter
- ¼ cup cooked ham cut in julienne strips
- ¼ cup cooked peas
- ¼ cup grated Parmesan cheese
- 2 well-beaten egg yolks

Cook noodles in boiling salted water about 5 minutes; drain. Meanwhile in large saucepan, combine cream, butter, ham, and peas; heat to melt butter. Stir in noodles. Cook about 5 minutes, till noodles are tender. Stir in cheese and egg yolks. Cook and stir till thickened slightly. Serves 4.

Valentino's
Santa Monica, California

Rigatoni ai 4 Formaggi
(Rigatoni with Four Cheeses)

- 12 ounces rigatoni
- 2 tablespoons butter
- 4 ounces Bel Paese cheese, shredded (1 cup)
- 4 ounces Fontina cheese, shredded (1 cup)
- 2 ounces Gorgonzola cheese, shredded (½ cup)
- 1 cup whipping cream
  Grated Parmesan cheese
  Ground pepper (optional)

Cook pasta according to package directions; drain. Meanwhile, in saucepan melt butter. Add Bel Paese, Fontina, and Gorgonzola cheeses, stirring till melted. Blend in cream. Place pasta on large platter; add sauce, tossing gently to coat. Sprinkle with Parmesan cheese and ground pepper. Serve at once. Makes 4 to 6 servings.

Taleggio alla Marinara con Acciughe

(Fried Cheese with Tomato Sauce)

- 1 large clove garlic, minced
- 1 tablespoon olive oil
- 5 medium tomatoes, peeled and chopped (1½ pounds)
- ½ 6-ounce can tomato paste (⅓ cup)
- ¼ cup Burgundy wine
- ½ teaspoon salt
- ½ teaspoon dried leaf basil, crushed
- ¼ teaspoon dried leaf oregano, crushed
- ⅛ teaspoon pepper

. . .

- 24 ounces Teleme *or* Mozzarella cheese
  Flour
- 4 well-beaten eggs
- ⅔ cup cracker meal
  Oil for deep frying
- 1 2-ounce can anchovy fillets, drained

Marinara Sauce: In 2-quart saucepan, cook garlic in olive oil till tender. Add tomatoes, tomato paste, Burgundy, salt, basil, oregano, and pepper. Bring to boil, stirring frequently. Reduce heat and boil gently, stirring often, till sauce is thickened, about 35 to 40 minutes. Keep warm.

Fried Cheese: Cut cheese into 3x2x½-inch pieces. Dip each piece in flour, then in eggs, then in cracker meal to coat all sides. Fry cheese a few pieces at a time in deep hot oil (375°) for 45 seconds to 1 minute, or till cheese is golden. Place each piece of cheese on small plate; top with one anchovy fillet and a spoonful of hot Marinara Sauce. Makes 6 appetizer servings.

‖Le Cordon Bleu

Belgian Chocolate Drink

  2 1-ounce squares unsweetened
     Belgian chocolate, grated
  1 cup hot strong coffee
  3 tablespoons sugar
     Dash salt
  3 cups milk
     Whipped cream

In saucepan, stir chocolate into coffee; add
sugar and salt. Stir in milk. Heat through but
do not boil. With rotary beater, beat until
frothy. Serve in cups topped with whipped
cream. Makes 4 servings. (Semisweet chocolate may be substituted.)

Green Pastures

Milk Punch

  2 cups vanilla ice cream
  1 cup milk
  ½ cup bourbon
  ¼ cup light rum
  3 tablespoons brandy
     Ground nutmeg

Stir ice cream to soften. Mix in remaining
ingredients. Serve in punch cups with a dash of
nutmeg on top. Makes 1 quart.

Moonkist Coconut

- ¾ cup light rum
- ¾ cup dark rum
- ⅓ cup milk
- ⅓ cup coconut syrup
- 2 tablespoons fresh lime juice
- 4 teaspoons honey
- 2 tablespoons sugar
    Several dashes aromatic bitters
- 2 cups crushed ice

Combine all ingredients in blender container; blend for 10 seconds. Pour over ice in glasses or coconut halves. Makes 4 servings.

Tintoretto

- 5 ounces chilled Champagne (about ⅔ cup)
- 2 ounces fresh pear, peeled, cored, and cut up (½ of medium pear)
- ½ ounce (1 tablespoon) pear brandy
    Lime slice

In blender container, combine Champagne, pear, and pear brandy. Blend till smooth. Pour into stemmed glass. Garnish with lime slice. Makes one drink.

RANCHO DEL RIO
THE TACK ROOM
Tucson, Arizona

Chilled Gazpacho Soup

      2 14½-ounce cans sliced baby tomatoes
      1 5¾-ounce can pitted black olives, sliced
     ¾ cup chopped celery
     ¾ cup chopped green onions
     ¾ cup chopped cucumber
      2 cloves garlic, minced
      3 tablespoons red wine vinegar
    1½ tablespoons beef gravy base
      1 teaspoon Worcestershire sauce
      6 drops bottled hot pepper sauce
      1 10½-ounce can condensed beef broth
     ¾ cup Chablis wine
        Chives, chopped
        Croutons

Drain tomatoes over a large bowl. Cut tomato slices into large pieces; add to juice in
bowl. Add olives, celery, green onion, cucum-
ber, and garlic. Stir in vinegar, beef gravy base,
Worcestershire sauce, hot pepper sauce, beef
broth, and wine; cover. Chill for 24 hours.
Ladle into chilled soup bowls; garnish with
chives and croutons. Makes 6 to 8 servings.

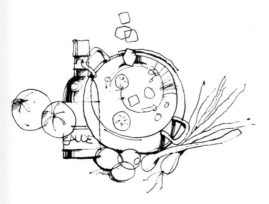

LONDON CHOP HOUSE

Detroit, Michigan

Watercress Soup

- 1 bunch watercress, stems removed (2 cups leaves)
- 1 cup chopped zucchini
- 1 cup chopped leeks
- 1 cup chopped, peeled potatoes
- ½ cup chopped Boston lettuce
- ½ cup snipped parsley (leaves and stems)
- ¼ cup sliced green onion
- 3 teaspoons chicken bouillon granules
- 2 cups water
- 1 cup whipping cream
  Dairy sour cream
  Green onion tops, finely cut
  Salt and pepper

In large saucepan, combine watercress, zucchini, leeks, potatoes, lettuce, parsley, the ¼ cup onion, and bouillon granules. Add water. Simmer, covered, for 10 to 15 minutes, till potatoes are tender. Pour half at a time into blender container; blend till very fine. Strain; discard vegetables. Season broth to taste with salt and pepper. Add whipping cream; heat through (do not boil).

Combine sour cream, green onion tops, and salt and pepper to taste; spoon atop each serving. Makes 4 servings.

Crème de Pois a L'Oseille
(Pea Soup and Sorrel)

- 1 tablespoon butter
- 1½ cups sorrel, cut up and lightly packed
- Dash salt
- Dash pepper
- Dash sugar
- 1 large leek, chopped (½ cup)
- 1 medium onion, chopped (½ cup)
- 2 tablespoons butter
- 1½ cups green split peas (10 ounces)
- 5 cups water
- 1 teaspoon salt
- 1 10½-ounce can beef consommé (1¼ cups)
- 2 cups whipping cream

In small saucepan, melt 1 tablespoon butter. Cook sorrel until completely dry. Season with dash salt, pepper, and sugar. In a 3-quart Dutch oven, cook leek and onion in 2 tablespoons butter till soft. Add peas, water, and the 1 teaspoon salt. Cover and cook in 375° oven until mixture is very soft, about 1½ hours, stirring occasionally.

Purée pea mixture; return to Dutch oven. Stir in beef consommé, cream, and sorrel. Heat through. Season to taste. Makes 6 servings.

Cheesey Chowder

    1   cup chopped onion
   ½   cup chopped carrot
   ½   cup chopped celery
    2   tablespoons butter
 1½   teaspoons paprika
    3   cups chicken broth
    6   ounces cheddar cheese, diced (1½ cups)
    6   ounces cold-pack cheese food (1½ cups)
   ½   cup light cream
   ⅓   cup all-purpose flour
    1   cup milk
   ½   teaspoon Worcestershire sauce
   ⅛   teaspoon pepper
        Grated Parmesan cheese

In heavy saucepan, cook onion, carrot, and celery in butter for 5 minutes. Blend in paprika. Add chicken broth. Bring to a boil; reduce heat, simmer, covered, 10 minutes. Add the cheeses; stir till melted. Add cream. Blend the flour with the milk; add to chowder. Cook and stir till slightly thickened. Add Worcestershire sauce and pepper. Ladle into soup bowls; sprinkle with grated Parmesan cheese. Put under broiler briefly to brown. Makes 4 to 6 servings.

La Caravelle

Crème Nouvelle France
(Cream of Corn Soup)

- ¼ cup chopped onion
- 1 tablespoon butter
- 1 tablespoon all-purpose flour
- 1 10-ounce package frozen corn
- 1 cup chicken broth
- 1 cup milk
- ½ cup whipping cream
- 1 tablespoon butter
- 1 5-ounce can lobster, drained and diced
- ⅓ cup bourbon

In medium saucepan, cook onion in 1 tablespoon butter till tender. Blend in flour. Reserve ½ cup of the corn. Add remaining corn and chicken broth to saucepan. Cover and simmer till corn is very tender, 30 minutes. Purée in blender or food processor; pass through sieve. Return to saucepan; add milk and cream. Heat through. Season to taste.

Meanwhile, in small saucepan, cook reserved corn in 1 tablespoon butter till tender, about 5 minutes. Add lobster and heat through. Remove to bowl. Add bourbon to saucepan, cooking and stirring up any loose particles in pan. Boil down to half. Pour over lobster mixture.

To serve: pour ¾ cup cream corn mixture in bowl; spoon ¼ cup lobster mixture in center. Makes 4 servings.

Old Original Bookbinder's Snapper Soup

1½   pounds veal knuckle, cut in 2-inch pieces
4   tablespoons butter
1   cup chopped onion
⅓   cup chopped celery
1   small carrot, chopped
¼   teaspoon thyme
    Dash marjoram
1   whole clove
1   bay leaf
½   teaspoon salt
¼   teaspoon pepper

.   .   .

¼   cup all-purpose flour
3   10½-ounce cans condensed beef broth
1   cup canned tomatoes
1   pound frozen snapper turtle meat,
    cut in small pieces
¾   cup water
½   cup dry sherry
    Dash bottled hot pepper sauce
1   slice lemon
1   hard-cooked egg, chopped

Place first 11 ingredients in shallow roasting pan. Bake at 400° for 30 minutes. Push bones to one side; blend in flour. Bake at 350° for 30 minutes longer. Transfer to kettle; add broth and tomatoes. Cover and simmer for 1½ hours.

Meanwhile, simmer turtle meat, covered, in ¾ cup water, 1 to 1½ hours, or till tender. Add sherry, hot pepper sauce, and lemon. Cover and simmer 10 minutes. Strain veal soup, discarding bones; skim off fat. Combine veal and turtle mixtures; stir in egg. Heat through. Season with salt and pepper. Makes 6 servings.

Bouillabaisse

- ½ cup sliced green onion
- ½ cup chopped celery
- ½ cup chopped anise root *or* ¼ teaspoon anise seed
- 1 clove garlic, minced
  Pinch Spanish saffron
- 2 tablespoons olive oil
- 3 cups fish stock
- 1 cup Chablis wine
- 1 cup dry sherry
- 1 6-ounce can tomato paste
- 1 crab, meat removed (about 2 pounds)
- 1 pound shrimp, peeled and deveined
- 12 ounces clams in shell, shelled
- ¾ pound halibut steak, cut in 1-inch pieces
- 1 lobster tail, peeled and cut in 1-inch pieces (½ pound)
- ½ pound snapper, skinned and cut in 1-inch pieces

In large saucepan, cook green onion, celery, anise, garlic, and saffron in olive oil till tender but not brown, about 5 minutes. Add fish stock, wines, and tomato paste. Heat to boiling; simmer 5 minutes. Add seafood. Simmer, covered, for 10 minutes or till seafood is done. Arrange seafood pieces on large platter. Serve with hot sauce. Makes 6 servings.

Gordon's

Oyster Chowder

- 1 pint oysters
- ½ cup finely chopped onion
- ¼ cup finely chopped celery
- ¼ cup finely chopped green pepper
- 2 tablespoons butter
- 1 cup light cream
- ½ of 8-ounce can (½ cup) tomato sauce
- 1 4-ounce can sliced mushrooms, drained
- ⅓ cup rice, cooked
- 2 tablespoons dry sherry
- 1 tablespoon snipped parsley
- ½ teaspoon salt
  Dash pepper
- ¼ teaspoon ground nutmeg

Drain oysters, reserving liquid; add water to liquid to make 1 cup. Chop oysters. In 2-quart saucepan simmer oysters in the liquid for 5 minutes, or till edges curl slightly. Remove from heat.

In another saucepan, cook onion, celery, and green pepper in butter till tender but not brown (6 to 8 minutes). Add to cooked oysters along with cream, tomato sauce, mushrooms, rice, sherry, parsley, salt, pepper, and nutmeg. Heat through. Season to taste. Serve immediately. Makes 4 servings.

Potage Lady Curzon

- 1 10-ounce can turtle soup
- 4 egg yolks
- ½ teaspoon curry powder
- 1 tablespoon dry sherry or port wine
  Salt and freshly ground pepper
- ½ cup whipping cream

In saucepan, bring turtle soup to boiling. In top of double boiler, heat together egg yolks, curry powder, and sherry. Gradually add boiling hot turtle soup. Cook and stir over hot water until soup thickens. Season to taste with salt and pepper. Ladle into cups at serving time.

Whip cream till stiffly beaten; spoon a dollop atop each cup. Place under broiler until lightly brown. Serve with Parmesan cheese straws. Makes 4 servings.

Chesapeake Restaurant

Baltimore, Maryland

Teriyaki Sauce Chesapeake
(Japanese Steak Sauce)

- ½ ounce shredded fresh gingerroot (2 tablespoons)
- 1 clove garlic, minced
- ⅓ cup sugar
- ¼ teaspoon monosodium glutamate
- ½ cup peach nectar
- ½ cup soy sauce
- Steak to serve 4 to 8

Combine ingredients in small bowl (do not use aluminum). Cover and refrigerate for 8 to 10 hours. Stir occasionally. Strain sauce. Cover and keep refrigerated for up to 2 to 3 weeks. Warm and serve hot over steaks. Makes 1¼ cups.

BACCHANAL

Steak Flambé Moutarde

  4 6-ounce pieces sirloin steak, cut 1 inch thick
  6 tablespoons butter
     Salt
     Pepper
¼ cup brandy
½ cup whipping cream
  3 tablespoons Dijon-style mustard
  2 tablespoons dairy sour cream
  1 teaspoon Worcestershire sauce

Pound pieces of steak between pieces of waxed paper to ½-inch thickness. In large skillet, heat butter and sauté sirloins for 2 minutes. Turn and season with salt and pepper. Cook to desired degree of doneness (2 minutes each side for rare). Pour brandy over steaks; ignite. When flame dies, transfer steaks to warm serving platter.

Add whipping cream, mustard, sour cream, and Worcestershire sauce to juices in pan. Cook and stir till heated through. Pour sauce over steaks to serve. Makes 4 servings.

Pepper Steak, Café de Paris

- 4 8-ounce sirloin steaks, 1 inch thick
  Salt
- 1 tablespoon whole black peppercorns, cracked
- 3 tablespoons butter
- 1 tablespoon whole black peppercorns, cracked
- ½ cup chopped shallots
- ¼ cup Cognac
- 1 tablespoon butter
- 1 tablespoon all-purpose flour
- ½ cup beef broth
- ½ cup whipping cream
- ¼ cup Cognac

Sprinkle steaks with salt. Press 1 tablespoon crushed peppercorns into both sides of the steaks. In large skillet, brown steaks quickly in 3 tablespoons of butter, about 2 to 3 minutes per side. Remove steaks to plate; sprinkle with 1 tablespoon peppercorns. Add shallots to skillet and cook till tender but not brown. Remove from heat. Add ¼ cup Cognac; ignite. When flame has gone out, replace skillet over heat. Add 1 tablespoon butter. Shake together flour and beef broth; add to skillet. Add cream; cook and stir till thickened and bubbly. Return steaks to skillet. Add ¼ cup Cognac. Cook, uncovered, over medium heat for 8 to 10 minutes, turning steaks once. Season to taste with salt. Makes 4 servings.

Filet de Boeuf en Croûte
(Beef Wellington)

- 1 10-ounce package frozen patty shells
- 1 4-pound beef tenderloin roast
  Salt
  All-purpose flour
- 2 cups fresh mushrooms, chopped
- 2 tablespoons butter
- 1 4½-ounce can goose liver paté
- 1 tablespoon Cognac
- 2 teaspoons snipped chives
  Salt
  Few grinds freshly ground pepper
- 1 egg yolk
- 1 tablespoon water

Allow patty shells to thaw 2 hours in refrigerator before rolling out. If meat is quite long, fold narrow end under to form a roast about 12 to 13 inches in length. Place on rack in shallow roasting pan. Sprinkle lightly with salt and flour. Bake, uncovered, in 425° oven till meat thermometer inserted in thickest portion registers 120°, about 35 to 40 minutes. Cool meat sufficiently to handle, about 20 minutes.

Meanwhile, in skillet, cook mushrooms in butter till tender, about 5 minutes. Remove from heat. Add paté, Cognac, and chives. Make a deep slit in center of roast, cutting from side, to but not through opposite side. Sprinkle pocket with salt and pepper. Spoon mushroom-paté mixture into pocket. On lightly floured surface arrange patty shells in a rectangle, overlapping edges slightly; press edges to seal. (If necessary, moisten edges with a little water.) Roll out to a 16x11-inch rectangle. Place roast in a greased 15x10x1-inch baking pan.

Lay pastry over roast, tucking under securely. Brush pastry with mixture of egg yolk and water. Bake in 425° oven for 20 minutes more, or till pastry is golden. Makes 8 servings.

Roast Filet of Beef-Pérgourdine

- ¼ cup all-purpose flour
- 1 2-pound beef tenderloin roast
- 2 tablespoons all-purpose flour
- ¼ teaspoon salt
- ⅛ teaspoon pepper
- ¼ cup cooking oil
- 2 tablespoons finely chopped onion
- 2 tablespoons finely chopped celery
- 2 tablespoons finely chopped carrot
- 1 teaspoon tomato paste
- 1 10½-ounce can condensed beef broth
- ¼ cup Madeira wine

Sprinkle the ¼ cup flour in 8x8x2-inch baking pan. Bake in 350° oven for 20 to 25 minutes till lightly browned, shaking pan occasionally.

Coat meat with mixture of the 2 tablespoons unbrowned flour, the salt, and pepper. Brown meat quickly in oil in 10-inch skillet. Remove meat to rack in shallow roasting pan. Reserve drippings in skillet.

Cook onion, celery, and carrot in drippings till tender, about 4 minutes. Blend in browned flour and tomato paste. Add beef broth. Cook and stir till thickened and bubbly. Add wine.

Strain sauce over meat in roasting pan. Roast, uncovered, in 425° oven for 45 minutes or till meat thermometer registers 140° for rare. Transfer roast to serving platter; spoon sauce atop. Garnish tenderloin with diced goose liver paté, truffles, and watercress, if desired. Makes 4 servings.

Steak Diane, Flambé

- 8 4-ounce beef tenderloin filets
  Salt and pepper
- 6 tablespoons clarified butter
- 8 ounces sliced mushrooms (3 cups)
- ¼ cup chopped shallots
- 1 tablespoon snipped parsley
- 1 teaspoon snipped chives
- ¼ cup Cognac
- ¼ cup condensed beef broth
- 2 tablespoons Madeira wine
- 2 tablespoons bottled Sauce Robert
- ½ teaspoon Worcestershire sauce
  Salt and pepper

Season meat with salt and pepper; set aside. Melt butter in blazer pan of chafing dish or in skillet over medium heat. Add mushrooms; cook 2 minutes. Add shallots, parsley, and chives; cook for 2 minutes more. Remove vegetables, reserving butter in pan. Increase heat. Cook half of the beef at a time in butter in same pan, 2 to 3 minutes per side for rare or medium rare.

Return vegetables and meat to pan. Add Cognac; flame. When flame is extinguished, add beef broth, wine, Sauce Robert, and Worcestershire sauce. Cook 1 minute, uncovered. Season to taste with salt and pepper. Makes 4 servings.

Tournedos of Beef Queen of Sheba

- 4 eggplant slices, peeled (¼ inch thick)
  All-purpose flour
- 4 tablespoons butter
- ¼ cup chopped shallots
- 2 tablespoons butter
- ½ cup beef broth
- 2 tablespoons white wine
- 2 tablespoons Burgundy wine
- 8 mushroom caps
- 16 asparagus tips
  Salt
  Pepper
- 4 4-ounce beef tenderloin filets
  All-purpose flour
- 4 ounces prosciutto ham, sliced
- ½ cup Hollandaise Sauce (page 2)

Dip eggplant slices lightly in flour. In 10-inch skillet cook eggplant in 4 tablespoons butter till browned on both sides, about 5 minutes. Remove and keep warm.

In same skillet, cook shallots in 2 tablespoons butter for 1 to 2 minutes. Stir in beef broth and wines. Add mushroom caps. Cover and cook 4 minutes more.

Cook asparagus in boiling salted water till tender. At same time salt and pepper pieces of tenderloin; dip in flour. Pan fry in hot fat to desired doneness, about 2 to 2½ minutes per side for rare.

For each serving, on a plate layer eggplant slices, prosciutto, and beef. Remove mushrooms from sauce; spoon about 1 tablespoon shallot sauce over tournedos. Top each with 2 mushroom caps. Pyramid asparagus on side with Hollandaise. Makes 4 servings.

Gah Lei Fon Ker Ngow Yuke

(Tomato Beef with Curry)

- ½ pound beef tenderloin or top round steak
- 2 tablespoons cooking oil
- Salt
- Pepper
- 2 medium onions, cut in ¾-inch wedges
- 1 small green pepper, cut in ¾-inch cubes
- ¼ cup chicken broth
- 1 tablespoon sugar
- 1 teaspoon curry powder
- ¼ teaspoon salt
- 1 tablespoon cornstarch
- 1 tablespoon cold water
- 3 tomatoes, cut in quarters
- Hot cooked rice

Partially freeze meat for ease in slicing. Slice meat into 2x1-inch pieces, about ¼-inch thick. Heat oil in wok or skillet. Add beef; sprinkle lightly with salt and pepper. Stir-fry 1 minute. Remove meat.

Add onions, green pepper, and chicken broth. Cover and cook 3 to 4 minutes over medium heat. Stir in sugar, curry, and ¼ teaspoon salt. Stir-fry 1 minute.

Blend together cornstarch and water; stir into wok. Cook and stir till thickened and bubbly. Add meat and tomatoes; heat through. Serve with hot rice. Makes 4 servings.

Shun Lee Dynasty

New York, New York

Hunan Beef

- ¾ pound beef flank steak
- 1 egg white
- 1 tablespoon cornstarch
- 2 tablespoons soy sauce
- 1 tablespoon chili paste with garlic (Szechuan paste)
- 1½ teaspoons cornstarch
- ½ teaspoon sugar
  Several drops sesame oil
- 2 cloves garlic, minced
- 3 to 4 tablespoons cooking oil
- 1 large bunch watercress (4 cups leaves)
- 1 tablespoon dry sherry
- ⅛ teaspoon salt

Partially freeze beef for ease in slicing. Slice, across grain, in thin slices. In bowl combine beef with egg white and 1 tablespoon cornstarch. Set aside.

In separate bowl, stir together soy sauce and chili paste; blend in 1½ teaspoons cornstarch, sugar, sesame oil, and garlic. Set aside.

Heat 2 tablespoons of the oil in wok or large skillet. Stir-fry meat, half at a time, 1½ to 2 minutes, adding additional tablespoon of oil if necessary. Return all meat to skillet. Add sauce mixture; cook and stir till thickened and bubbly. Remove meat to one side of a warm platter; keep warm.

Wipe wok clean. Heat remaining 1 tablespoon oil; add watercress, sherry, and salt. Stir-fry 30 to 45 seconds. Arrange watercress on other side of platter. Makes 4 servings.

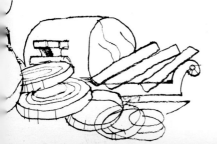

Cafe Johnell

Fort Wayne, Indiana

Truite Soufflé
(Trout Soufflé)

     4 boneless 8-ounce trout
     4 egg whites
  ½ teaspoon salt
  ¼ teaspoon pepper
       Dash ground nutmeg
1½ cups whipping cream
       Butter, melted
       Paprika
       Parsley
       Lemon

       .   .   .

     4 tablespoons butter
  ¼ cup tomato juice
     3 tablespoons lemon juice

With a sharp knife, carefully remove fish from skin, leaving head, tail, and skin intact. Put trout through grinder. In large mixer bowl, combine egg whites, salt, pepper, and nutmeg with ground fish; beat at medium-high speed of electric mixer until thickened to a paste. Add cream; whip at low speed until mixture starts to thicken, then gradually increase speed to high, until mixture resembles dough.

Stuff one-fourth the mixture into each trout skin so that fish resume original shape. Refrigerate till needed. To cook, place on greased pan. Brush with butter and sprinkle lightly with paprika. Bake in 450° oven for 15 minutes. Trout will puff up. Remove; garnish with parsley and lemon. Pour sauce over and serve. Makes 4 servings.

Sauce: In small saucepan, melt 4 tablespoons butter; cool. Pour off clear top layer; discard solids in bottom. Return clear portion to small saucepan; heat slowly till a light brown. Add tomato juice and lemon juice; heat through.

Truite Talloires
(Trout Talloires)

8	ounces fresh mushrooms (about 3 cups)
2	tablespoons lemon juice
¼	teaspoon Worcestershire sauce
½	teaspoon salt
	Dash pepper
⅛	teaspoon leaf thyme, crushed
2	tablespoons dry white wine
2	tablespoons white wine vinegar
1	teaspoon shallots, finely chopped
½	teaspoon leaf tarragon, crushed
½	teaspoon chervil, crushed
⅛	teaspoon coarsely ground black pepper
	Dash cayenne
4	egg yolks
½	cup butter, softened
4	trout, boned, head and tail removed (about 8 ounces each)
½	cup all-purpose flour
½	teaspoon salt
	Dash pepper
3	tablespoons cooking oil
1	cup soft bread crumbs (about 1½ slices)
1	tablespoon butter, melted

Finely chop mushrooms. In small skillet, combine mushrooms, lemon juice, Worcestershire sauce, salt, pepper, and thyme; cook, uncovered, till all liquid is evaporated, about 6 to 8 minutes. Cover and set aside.

In small saucepan, combine white wine, vinegar, shallots, tarragon, chervil, coarse pepper, and cayenne; boil gently till all but 2 tablespoons liquid is evaporated. Add to egg yolks in top of double boiler; stir to blend yolks. Place pan with yolks over, but not touching, boiling water. Stirring constantly, add ½ cup butter a few tablespoons at a time till all is added. Continue cooking and stirring till thick ened. Remove from heat; cover and place over a bowl of warm water to keep warm.

Remove any fins from trout being sure not to separate fillets. Coat both sides of each trout with mixture of flour, ½ teaspoon salt, and dash pepper. In large skillet, brown two at a time in hot oil, about 4 to 5 minutes per side. Keep browned trout warm.

Place trout skin side down on ovenproof platter or baking pan. Spread each trout with 2 tablespoons of the mushroom purée. Combine bread crumbs and melted butter; sprinkle atop mushroom purée on each trout. Broil 3 to 5 inches from heat for 1 to 2 minutes or till crumbs are golden. Serve with warm sauce. Makes 4 servings.

THE FOUR SEASONS

New York, New York

A Baked Tartar of Red Snapper and Bay Scallops

1½ pounds red snapper fillets, skinned
   8 ounces scallops
   2 teaspoons green peppercorns
   4 tablespoons unsalted butter, softened
   2 tablespoons olive oil
   1 tablespoon Cognac or Armagnac
   2 teaspoons salt
   ¼ teaspoon sweetened lime juice
   ½ cup fine dry bread crumbs
   ¾ cup whipping cream

Coarsely grind red snapper and scallops together. Chop peppercorns; mash. Add to fish mixture along with butter, olive oil, Cognac, salt, and lime juice. Mix well. Shape into 6 patties, about 3x3 inches. Coat with bread crumbs; place in gratin dishes. Sprinkle with a few whole green peppercorns, a little paprika and dot with butter. Pour 2 tablespoons cream around each fish patty, being careful not to moisten bread crumbs on top. Bake in 350° oven for 12 to 15 minutes, till done. Serves 6.

L'Epuisette

Chicago, Illinois

Stuffed Boneless Brook Trout

- 2 10-ounce rainbow trout, cleaned
- 2 tablespoons butter
- ½ cup chopped fresh mushrooms
- ½ teaspoon chopped shallots
- ½ teaspoon snipped chives
- 2 tablespoons butter
- 1 tablespoon all-purpose flour
- ¼ cup milk
- ⅛ teaspoon salt
- Dash pepper
- 2 tablespoons dry white wine
- 6 ounces king crab meat, chopped (1 cup)
- Lemon juice

Cook trout in 2 tablespoons butter until browned on both sides, about 4 to 5 minutes per side. Remove from pan. Working from the belly side, carefully bone the trout. Keep warm.

In small saucepan, cook mushrooms, shallots, and chives in 2 tablespoons butter till tender, about 1½ minutes. Blend in flour. Add milk, salt, and pepper. Cook and stir till thickened and bubbly. Stir in wine. Add crab meat. Heat through till crab is cooked.

Place the trout on serving platter; fill each with crab meat mixture. Sprinkle the tops with a little lemon juice. Makes 2 servings.

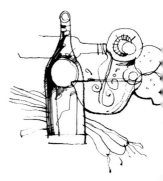

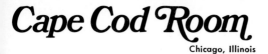

Pompano-Papillote à la Drake

- 1 cup sliced fresh mushrooms
- 1 tablespoon chopped shallots
- 2 tablespoons butter
- ¾ cup dry red wine
- ¾ cup water
- ½ teaspoon salt
- ½ teaspoon Worcestershire sauce
- 6 7-ounce pompano fillets
- 1 tablespoon all-purpose flour
- 2 tablespoons cold water
- 1 5-ounce can lobster, drained and diced
  Oiled parchment paper

In 12-inch skillet, cook mushrooms and shallots in butter. Stir in wine, ¾ cup water, salt, and Worcestershire. Add fish fillets to skillet. Bring to boiling; reduce heat. Cover and simmer, 4 to 5 minutes or just till fish is done. Remove fish.

Boil pan liquid hard till reduced to ¾ cup. Blend flour and 2 tablespoons water. Stir into the ¾ cup liquid in skillet. Cook and stir till thickened and bubbly. Stir in lobster.

Cut six large valentine hearts from parchment paper, about 18 inches long by 14 inches wide. Brush top side with oil. Place one fish fillet on left half of heart; top with some of the lobster sauce. Repeat with remaining fillets. Fold the right half of paper heart over the fillet, turning all edges to form a tight seal. Bake in 350° oven for 10 to 15 minutes till bags begin to puff. Makes 6 servings.

Sole Vanessi

    6 3-ounce sole fillets
       Salt
    3 slices Swiss cheese, halved lengthwise
       (4x7-inch slices, 4 ounces)
    1 6-ounce package or 7-ounce can crab meat
  ½ teaspoon dried basil, crushed
    6 mushroom caps
    2 teaspoons butter
    2 tablespoons chopped mushrooms
  ½ teaspoon chopped shallots
    1 teaspoon lemon juice
    3 tablespoons dry white wine
    2 tablespoons clarified butter
    3 tablespoons all-purpose flour
    1 cup fish stock
  ⅓ cup light cream
  ½ teaspoon lemon juice
       Salt

Place fish on waxed paper and sprinkle lightly
with salt. On each sole fillet place one-half
cheese slice, 1 ounce crab meat, a sprinkle of
basil, and a mushroom cap. Roll up and place
seam side down in 12x7½x2-inch baking dish.
Set aside.

In saucepan, cook 2 teaspoons butter,
chopped mushrooms, shallots, and 1 teaspoon
lemon juice till mushrooms are tender. Add
wine and cook till almost evaporated. Add clarified butter and flour; mix well. Add fish stock;
cook and stir till thickened and bubbly. Add
cream, ½ teaspoon lemon juice, and season to
taste with salt. Strain. Pour sauce atop fish rolls.
If desired, sprinkle with paprika. Cover and
bake in 400° oven for 25 to 30 minutes. Makes
6 servings.

Soufflé de Sole Anglaise
(Soufflé of English Sole)

- 12 ounces fresh or frozen skinless sole fillets, thawed and cut up
- 2 tablespoons butter
- 2 tablespoons all-purpose flour
- ½ teaspoon salt
- ⅛ teaspoon pepper
- ½ cup fish stock
- ½ cup light cream
- 4 egg yolks
- 4 egg whites

Put fish through food processor or fine blade of food grinder; set aside. In saucepan, melt butter; blend in flour, salt, and pepper. Add stock and cream. Cook and stir till thickened and bubbly. Remove from heat; stir in ground fish; set aside.

Beat egg yolks till thick and lemon-colored, about 5 minutes; fold in fish mixture. Beat egg whites to stiff peaks; fold in yolk mixture. Turn into 2-quart soufflé dish. Bake in 350° oven for 40 to 45 minutes, or till knife inserted off-center comes out clean. Makes 4 servings.

Sole Albert
(Sole Baked with Vermouth)

- ½ cup dry vermouth
- 4 tablespoons butter, melted
- 3 chopped shallots (4 teaspoons)
- 1 tablespoon snipped parsley
- ½ teaspoon dried tarragon, crushed
- 1½ cups soft bread crumbs (2 slices)
- 2 tablespoons butter, melted
- 6 sole fillets (1½ pounds)
- ½ teaspoon lemon juice

In 13x9x2-inch baking dish, combine vermouth, the 4 tablespoons melted butter, the shallots, parsley, and tarragon; spread evenly in dish. Combine bread crumbs and remaining melted butter. Sprinkle over fish. Place fish, crumb side up, atop butter mixture. Bake in 425° oven for 15 minutes, or till fish flakes easily with a fork. Remove fillets to serving plates. Strain juices. Stir in lemon juice; pour over each serving of fish. Makes 6 servings.

Flounder Stuffed with Deviled Crab

- ¼ cup chopped onion
- 1 tablespoon butter
- ¼ cup mayonnaise
- 1 tablespoon vinegar
- 1 tablespoon Worcestershire sauce
- ½ teaspoon dry mustard
- ¼ teaspoon salt
- 1 cup firm-textured bread crumbs, crusts removed (3 slices)
- 2 hard-cooked eggs, chopped
- 8 ounces fresh crab meat, flaked *or* 1 7½-ounce can crab meat, drained and flaked
- 4 flounder fillets (1½ pounds)
- 1 tablespoon butter, melted

In saucepan, cook onion in 1 tablespoon butter till tender but not brown. In bowl, blend together mayonnaise, vinegar, Worcestershire, mustard, and salt. Stir in bread crumbs, onion, and eggs. Fold in crab. Spread ⅓ to ½ cup filling on one side of each fillet. Roll up. Place seam side down in 8x8x2-inch baking pan. Brush with melted butter. Bake in 375° oven for 30 to 35 minutes. Place under broiler briefly until golden brown. Makes 4 servings.

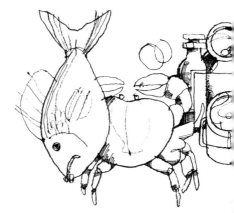

Rouget Grillé Beurre Nantaise
(Red Snapper with Butter Nantaise)

- ¼ teaspoon salt
  Dash pepper
- ¼ teaspoon dried thyme
- 1 small bay leaf, crumbled
- 1 tablespoon lemon juice
- 1 red snapper, cleaned (3 pounds)
  Cooking oil
- ⅛ teaspoon salt
- ¼ teaspoon dried thyme
  . . .
- ¼ cup shallots, chopped
- ¼ cup white vinegar
- ¼ cup white wine
- 1½ cups whipping cream

Combine salt, pepper, ¼ teaspoon thyme, bay leaf, and lemon juice. Rub in inside of cavity of fish. Rub outside of fish with a little oil and sprinkle with salt and ¼ teaspoon thyme. Place in greased baking pan. Bake in 350° oven for 45 to 60 minutes. Makes 2 servings.

Beurre Nantaise: In small pan, combine shallots, vinegar, and wine. Bring to boiling; boil till reduced to 3 tablespoons. Discard solids. In a 3-quart saucepan, boil cream till reduced to ¾ cup. Add strained wine liquid. Serve with fish.

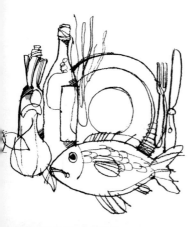

India House

San Francisco, California

Lamb Curry Khorma

    3 medium onions, chopped (2½ cups)
    1 clove garlic, minced
   ¼ cup cooking oil
   ½ teaspoon ground coriander
   ½ teaspoon dillweed
   ⅛ teaspoon ground mace
   ⅛ teaspoon ground ginger
   ⅛ teaspoon cayenne
   ⅛ teaspoon ground nutmeg
   ½ cup water
    1 tablespoon cumin seed
    3 pods cardamom seeds, opened
    3 bay leaves
    3 whole cloves
    1 inch stick cinnamon
    2 pounds shoulder lamb, fat removed, cut in
       1-inch cubes
    2 teaspoons turmeric
    1 teaspoon salt
   ⅛ teaspoon pepper

In 3-quart saucepan, cook onions and garlic in oil, covered, for 10 minutes. Add coriander, dillweed, mace, ginger, cayenne, and nutmeg. Cook, covered, 10 minutes longer.

In small saucepan, combine water, cumin seed, cardamom seeds, bay leaves, cloves, and cinnamon; simmer, covered, for 10 minutes. Strain. Discard seeds. Add liquid to onions. Roll lamb in turmeric. Add to onions along with salt and pepper. Cover and cook about 30 minutes or till tender. Makes 6 servings.

Carré d' Agneau en Croûte
(Rack of Lamb in Pastry)

8 frozen patty shells
4 4-rib lamb chops (about 8 ounces each)
2 tablespoons butter
¼ cup Dijon-style mustard
½ cup fine dry bread crumbs
½ teaspoon garlic powder

Thaw patty shells in refrigerator two hours. Brown lamb on both sides in hot butter. Cool slightly. Spread each portion of lamb with 1 tablespoon mustard.

Combine bread crumbs and garlic; sprinkle over lamb, coating all sides. Roll two patty shells to 9-inch square. Wrap around one lamb portion, cutting around the bones and leaving them exposed. Repeat with remaining shells and lamb. Place on ungreased baking sheet. Bake in 400° oven for 20 to 25 minutes. Makes 4 servings.

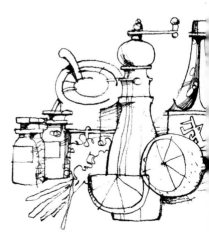

ray's ray's ray's

Marinated Lamb

- 2 cups dry red wine
- 1 tablespoon salt
- 1 tablespoon dried oregano
- 1 tablespoon dried thyme
- 2 teaspoons coarse pepper
- ¼ cup chopped onion
- ¼ cup chopped parsley
- 3 tablespoons soy sauce
- 2 tablespoons lemon juice
- 1 8-bone rack of lamb with back fat removed
  or 8 lamb chops

Combine wine, salt, oregano, thyme, and coarse pepper. Stir in onion, parsley, soy sauce, and lemon juice. Place rack of lamb or chops in container; pour marinade atop. Refrigerate overnight (for rack) or several hours (for chops), turning lamb occasionally. Remove meat from marinade. Slice between bones of rack. Grill over medium coals for approximately 25 minutes, turning occasionally. Serves 4.

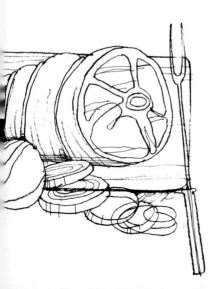

Rack of Lamb with Cream Garlic Sauce

  1 8-rib rack of lamb (2½ to 3 pounds —
double set of connected ribs)
Salt
Pepper

  . . .

  4 ounces lamb bones
  1 stalk celery, cut up (½ cup)
  1 small carrot, cut up (⅓ cup)
½ small onion, cut up (2 tablespoons)
  2 cloves garlic, minced
  1 cup water
  2 tablespoons dry sherry
  1 small bay leaf
⅛ teaspoon dried rosemary

  1 tablespoon butter, softened
  1 tablespoon all-purpose flour
¼ cup whipping cream
⅛ teaspoon salt

Remove fell from lamb. Place roast, fat side up, in shallow roasting pan; sprinkle with salt and pepper. Roast, uncovered, in 400° oven for 45 to 50 minutes or till meat thermometer registers 175°. Spoon off fat as it accumulates.

Cream Garlic Sauce: In 1½-quart saucepan combine lamb bones, celery, carrot, onion, garlic, water, sherry, bay leaf, and rosemary. Boil gently, uncovered for 15 to 20 minutes, or till liquid is reduced by about ⅔. Strain, reserving liquid (should have ⅓ cup broth). Place broth in small saucepan.

Stir together softened butter and flour till smooth. Add to broth in saucepan. Cook and stir till thickened and bubbly. Stir in whipping cream and the ⅛ teaspoon salt; heat through. Serve with roast. Makes 2 servings.

**Charlie's
cafe exceptionale**

Minneapolis, Minnesota

Braised Viennese Pork Roast

    1 3-pound boneless pork loin roast
    ¼ cup bacon drippings
    1 cup chopped onion
    1 cup chopped carrot
    1 teaspoon paprika
    ¾ cup chicken broth
    2 tablespoons all-purpose flour
    ½ cup dairy sour cream
    ¼ teaspoon caraway seed
    1 teaspoon chopped capers
    1 tablespoon snipped parsley

In ovenproof skillet or Dutch oven, brown pork loin roast in bacon drippings; set aside. In remaining drippings, cook onion and carrot till tender but not brown. Stir in paprika. Lay roast atop vegetables; add chicken broth. Bake, covered, in 350° oven for 1½ to 2 hours, or till meat thermometer registers 170°. Remove roast to serving platter; keep warm.

Strain pan drippings; discard vegetables. Measure pan drippings; skim off excess fat. Add water to drippings, if necessary, to measure 1⅓ cups. Return to skillet or Dutch oven. Blend flour into sour cream; stir into liquid in pan. Cook and stir till thickened and bubbly. Stir in caraway seed, capers, and parsley. Serve with roast. Makes 6 servings.

Grilled and Steamed Chiao Tzu

(Pot Stickers)

- 4 ounces prawns or shrimp, cooked, peeled, deveined, and finely chopped
- 4 ounces lean pork, finely chopped
- ⅓ cup Chinese cabbage, finely chopped
- 2 tablespoons green onions with tops, finely sliced
- 1 tablespoon chopped fresh coriander or cilantro
- 1 teaspoon grated fresh gingerroot
- 2 teaspoons sesame oil
- 2 tablespoons soy sauce
- 1 tablespoon chicken broth
- 2⅓ cups all-purpose flour
- ½ teaspoon salt
- 1 cup cold water
- 2 tablespoons cooking oil
- 2 teaspoons sesame oil
- 1 cup water

Combine prawns, pork, and Chinese cabbage. Add onions, coriander, gingerroot, 2 teaspoons sesame oil, soy sauce, and broth. Mix well. Cover and refrigerate at least 1 hour.

Meanwhile, combine flour, salt, and 1 cup water. Work by hand until smooth. Dust with flour. Place under inverted bowl and let rest at room temperature 30 minutes. Divide dough in 3 portions. On a well-floured surface, roll each portion out to ⅛-inch thickness. Using 3-inch cutter, cut into 12 rounds, rolling as needed.

Spoon 1 rounded teaspoon filling in center of each round. Fold rounds in half across filling and pinch edges to seal. Set pinched edge of dumpling upright and press gently to flatten bottom. Transfer to baking sheet. Cover with dry towel.

In 10-inch skillet, heat 1 tablespoon oil and 1 teaspoon sesame oil. Add half of the dumplings, arranging so they do not touch. Cook 1 minute or till bottoms are lightly browned. Add ½ cup of the remaining water. Cover and cook 6 minutes, till water has evaporated.

Using wide spatula, gently remove from skillet. Keep warm while cooking remaining dumplings with remaining 1 tablespoon cooking oil, 1 teaspoon sesame oil, and ½ cup water. Makes 36 dumplings.

Dearborn, Michigan

Dipping Sauces
(Sauces ideal with pork)

1½ tablespoons orange juice
1½ tablespoons catsup
1 tablespoon soy sauce
1½ tablespoons prepared horseradish
¼ cup dry mustard
1 slice onion
½ medium green pepper, cut up
1 clove garlic, sliced
1 tablespoon lime juice

. . .

½ cup soy sauce
½ cup vinegar
1 tablespoon grated fresh gingerroot
2 teaspoons lemon juice
½ teaspoon grated onion

Chili Dipping Sauce: In blender container, place orange juice, catsup, 1 tablespoon soy sauce, horseradish, dry mustard, onion slice, green pepper, garlic, and lime juice. Blend thoroughly. Makes ⅔ cup.

Ginger Dipping Sauce: In small bowl, combine ½ cup soy sauce, vinegar, ginger, lemon juice, and grated onion. Makes 1 cup.

Serve in small dipping bowl with meat, seafood, and vegetables.

Quiche Michele

   1 cup fresh mushrooms, sliced
 ½ cup diced ham
   2 tablespoons butter
   2 beaten eggs
   1 cup whipping cream
 ½ cup shredded cheddar cheese (2 ounces)
 ¼ teaspoon ground nutmeg
 ½ teaspoon salt
     Dash pepper
   1 9-inch baked quiche or pie shell

In saucepan, cook mushrooms and ham in butter till mushrooms are tender, about 5 minutes. Set aside. In mixing bowl, combine eggs, cream, cheese, nutmeg, salt, and pepper. Place ham-mushroom mixture in bottom of baked shell; pour egg mixture atop. Bake in 350° oven for 25 minutes. Let stand 10 minutes before serving. Makes one 9-inch quiche.

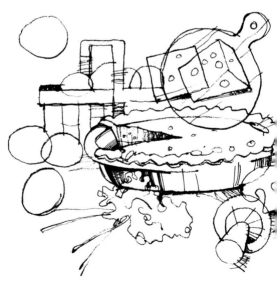

Pork Medallions, à la Lida Lee

- 1 whole pork tenderloin (about 12 ounces)
  All-purpose flour
- 3 tablespoons clarified butter
  Salt
  Pepper
  Curry powder
- 3 medium mushrooms, quartered
- 2 tablespoons dry sherry
- 2 tablespoons brown sauce
- 2 tablespoons light cream
- ½ tomato, peeled and chopped
  Chives

Cut tenderloin into 4 pieces. Pound thin and coat lightly with flour. In large skillet, cook slowly in clarified butter till well browned on one side. Sprinkle with salt, pepper, and curry. Turn; sprinkle meat with the seasonings. Add mushrooms and cook till tenderloin is browned on other side. Remove to platter and keep warm.

To skillet, add sherry, brown sauce, light cream, and tomato. Stir well to scrape up browned bits. Pour sauce over medallions on platter. Garnish with fresh cut chives. Makes 2 servings.

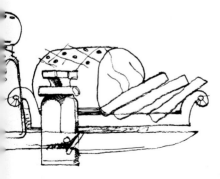

the pink adobe

Poulet Marengo Pink Adobe
(Chicken Marengo)

- 1 cup all-purpose flour
- 4 teaspoons salt
- 1 teaspoon paprika
- 3 2½- to 3-pound broiler-fryer chickens, cut in half lengthwise
- 2 tablespoons butter
- 2 tablespoons olive oil
- 1½ teaspoons bouquet garni
- 1 16-ounce can tomatoes, cut up
- 1 16-ounce can whole onions, drained
- ½ cup Madeira wine
- ½ cup pitted ripe olives
- 6 large whole mushrooms
- 1 clove garlic, minced
- 1 bay leaf
- ½ cup all-purpose flour
- 1 cup chicken broth
- 1 4½-ounce can paté of foie gras
- 6 cooked shrimp, chopped (1 cup)
- ½ cup small croutons

Combine 1 cup flour, salt, and paprika; coat both sides of chicken halves. In large skillet, brown chicken halves two at a time in the hot butter and oil. Sprinkle with bouquet garni.

In bowl, combine tomatoes, onions, Madeira, olives, mushrooms, garlic, and bay leaf. Place three of the chicken halves in bottom of roaster; pour half the tomato mixture over all. Repeat with remaining chicken halves and tomato mixture. Cover, bake in 325° oven for 2 hours.

Remove chicken, onions, mushrooms, and olives to platter; keep warm. Spoon off fat; measure 3 cups pan juices. Return to roasting pan. Combine the ½ cup flour and chicken broth; add to juices in roaster. Cook and stir till thickened and bubbly. Spread chicken halves with paté; top with shrimp and a few croutons. Pass the sauce. Makes 6 servings.

Coq Sauté au Riesling d'Alsace
(Chicken sautéed in Riesling)

- 1   2½- to 3-pound broiler-fryer chicken, cut up
  Salt and pepper
- 2   tablespoons butter
- 1   medium onion, chopped (½ cup)
- 1   clove garlic, minced
- 1   bay leaf
- 2   whole cloves
- 1   cup Riesling or dry white Alsatian wine
- ½   cup water
- 1   cup whipping cream
- 2   tablespoons all-purpose flour
- 3   beaten egg yolks
  Dash ground nutmeg
  Salt and pepper
  Hot cooked noodles

Sprinkle chicken pieces with salt and pepper. In large 12-inch skillet, slowly brown chicken in the 2 tablespoons butter (about 10 minutes). Add onion, garlic, bay leaf, cloves, wine, and water. Bring to boil; reduce heat. Cover and simmer till chicken is tender, about 30 minutes.

Remove chicken pieces to platter; keep warm. Discard bay leaf and cloves. Skim excess fat from pan juices. Quickly boil pan juices and onion, uncovered, till reduced to 1¼ cups. Strain juices, discard onion pieces; set aside.

Shake together whipping cream and flour. In saucepan, combine whipping cream mixture, pan juices, egg yolks, and nutmeg; cook and stir till thickened but do not boil. Season to taste with salt and pepper. Serve chicken and sauce over hot noodles. Makes 4 servings.

Cotelette à la Kiev

(Chicken Kiev)

- ½ pound butter
- 2 large chicken breasts with wing bone attached
  Salt
  Pepper
- 1 cup all-purpose flour
- 1 beaten egg
- 1 cup dry white bread crumbs
  Oil for deep frying

Cut the 2 sticks of butter into 4 equal parts. Shape each piece of butter into a cylinder about three inches long. Wrap in waxed paper and chill.

Skin, bone and halve the chicken breasts. Place the 4 halved breasts, smooth side down, on cutting board. With your fingers remove the small fillet (next to breast bone area). With a sharp knife, remove as much of joint holding the wing bone as possible without detaching the bone. Butterfly each ½ breast by cutting partially through the flesh from the center to each side. Lay the breasts and fillets on a sheet of waxed paper. With the flat side of a cleaver or metal meat pounder, pound them flat. If holes appear in the flesh, overlap the edges of the tear, slightly cover patch with waxed paper and pound gently until meat joins together.

To assemble the cutlets, gently peel off waxed paper and sprinkle chicken with salt and pepper. Wrap the chicken breasts around the chilled butter sticks. Be sure no butter is exposed. Push wing bone into butter then wrap fillet around the base of the protruding bone as you would a scarf.

In small bowl, beat eggs enough to combine. Spread flour and bread crumbs on two separate strips of waxed paper. Dip cutlets into flour, shaking gently to remove excess. With the palms of your hands, pat the cutlet into a long cylinder, tapering it slightly at each end. Dip cutlets into eggs and then into bread crumbs. Repeat procedure by dipping into egg and bread crumbs again. Chill for 1 to 2 hours.

Fry chicken rolls in deep hot oil (365°) about 5 minutes, till golden brown. Then place in 400° oven for no longer than 10 minutes. Garnish with chopped dill, if desired. Makes 4 servings.

RESTAURANT   Chicago, Illinois

Roast Duckling with Cherry Glaze

4½-to-5-pound duckling
- 3 tablespoons Chef's Salt*
- 3 tablespoons lard
- 2 stalks celery, coarsely chopped (⅔ cup)
- 1 carrot, coarsely chopped (½ cup)
- 1 small onion, chopped
- 2 cloves garlic, thinly sliced
- 3 to 4 black peppercorns
- 2 small bay leaves, crumbled
- ¼ teaspoon dried marjoram, crushed

- 1 16-ounce can pitted sour cherries, undrained
- ¼ cup sugar
- 4 inches stick cinnamon
- 1 slice lemon peel, ½x½-inch
- ½ cup dry red wine
- 1 tablespoon cold water
- 1 tablespoon cornstarch

66

Rinse and dry duck. Rub inside and out with Chef's Salt. Place lard in roasting pan with tight-fitting cover. In bowl, combine celery, carrot, onion, garlic, peppercorns, bay leaves, and marjoram. Place some in duck cavity. Place duck, breast down, on lard. Place remaining vegetable mixture around duck. Add water to depth of 2 inches. Cover and roast in 325° oven for 2 to 2½ hours. Remove from pan and cool completely. Quarter duck. Place skin side up in 15x10x1-inch pan. Bake in 425° oven for 20 to 22 minutes.

Glaze: In blender container, combine half the cherries and half the cherry juice. Blend until smooth. Place in saucepan with remaining cherries, juice, sugar, cinnamon, and peel. Bring to boil and boil 3 minutes. Add wine; return to boil. Remove from heat. Cover and let steep 5 minutes. Blend water and cornstarch. Add to cherry mixture. Cook and stir till thickened and bubbly. Remove cinnamon and peel. Serve warm or cold with duck. Makes 4 servings.

*****Chef's Salt:** Combine ½ cup salt, 1½ teaspoons Spanish or Hungarian paprika, 1½ teaspoons ground black pepper, ⅛ teaspoon white pepper, ⅛ teaspoon celery salt, ⅛ teaspoon garlic salt. Mix well. Use 3 tablespoons. Store remainder for other uses.

Ballotines de Volaille

(Stuffed Chicken Bundles)

- 12 ounces boneless veal sirloin steak
- 2 tablespoons olive oil
- 1 tablespoon dry sherry
- 2 ounces pork fat
- 1 teaspoon spiced salt*
- 4 whole chicken breasts, skinned and boned
- 1 tablespoon butter, melted
- 4 canned peach halves
- 2 tablespoons butter
- ¼ cup port wine
- 3 tablespoons dry sherry
- 2 tablespoons chopped mushroom stems
- ½ cup condensed beef broth
- 1 tablespoon all-purpose flour

Cut 8 ounces of the veal in julienne strips. Brown strips in olive oil; remove and set aside. Add 1 tablespoon sherry to skillet and cook, stirring up brown bits. Combine sherry and drippings with pork fat, remaining 4 ounces veal, and 1 teaspoon spiced salt; grind together.

Pound chicken breasts flat to about 7x6 inches. Sprinkle lightly with salt. Spread each breast with ¼ of the ground veal mixture. Place julienne strips of veal atop. Roll into ball shape, folding sides in. Brush with 1 tablespoon melted butter. Place in 9x9x2-inch baking pan. Bake, uncovered, in 350° oven for 30 minutes or till done.

Meanwhile, in skillet, cook peach halves in 2 tablespoons butter; remove and set aside. Add port wine, 3 tablespoons sherry, and mushroom stems. Cook to reduce by half. Blend beef broth and flour; stir into wine mixture. Cook and stir till thickened and bubbly. Serve each ballotine with peach on top and sauce. Serves 4.

***Spiced Salt:** Combine 1 tablespoon salt, 1½ teaspoons ground allspice, 1 teaspoon pepper.

Poitrine de Poularde Bombay

(Breast of Capon in Curry)

- 4 whole capon *or* chicken breasts, split, skinned, and boned
- ¼ cup all-purpose flour
- ½ teaspoon salt
- ⅛ teaspoon pepper
- ¼ teaspoon curry powder
- 4 tablespoons butter
- 2 small bananas, sliced (about 1¼ cups)
- 1 medium apple, peeled and chopped (1 cup)
- ½ cup chopped celery
- ¼ cup chopped onion
- 2 teaspoons curry powder
- 1 13¾-ounce can clear chicken broth (1¾ cups)
- ¼ cup dry white wine
- 2 tablespoons butter, softened
- 2 tablespoons all-purpose flour
- ½ teaspoon salt
- ⅛ teaspoon pepper
- ¼ cup whipping cream
- 1 8-ounce can pineapple slices, drained and halved crosswise
  Toasted coconut

Coat capon breasts with a mixture of the ¼ cup flour, the ½ teaspoon salt, the first ⅛ teaspoon pepper, and the ¼ teaspoon curry powder. In 12-inch skillet, slowly brown capon on both sides in the 4 tablespoons butter (about 10 minutes). Remove capon and set aside, reserving drippings in skillet.

Cook banana, apple, celery, onion, and the 2 teaspoons curry powder in skillet drippings till vegetables are tender but not brown. Add chicken broth and wine to skillet along with capon breasts. Cover and simmer 40 minutes or till tender.

Remove capon to deep heat-proof platter;

keep warm. Combine the 2 tablespoons softened butter, 2 tablespoons flour, ½ teaspoon
salt, and ⅛ teaspoon pepper to form a smooth
paste; add to skillet mixture. Cook and stir till
thickened and bubbly. Add cream and pineapple slices; heat through.

Pour sauce over capon on platter. Broil 4 to
5 inches from heat for 4 to 5 minutes or till
surface is golden. Sprinkle with toasted coconut. Serve with rice pilaf and chutney. Makes
8 servings.

TOLL GATE LODGE

Manchester, Vermont

Supreme of Capon Smitane

  6 whole capon *or* chicken breasts, skinned
     and boned
     Butter, melted
½ cup chopped onion
  2 tablespoons butter
  1 cup dry white wine
  2 tablespoons all-purpose flour
½ cup milk
  1 cup sour cream
  1 tablespoon chicken extract
¼ teaspoon salt
     Dash pepper
  2 tablespoons lemon juice
     Hot cooked wild rice

Place capon breasts in shallow pan. Brush with
a little melted butter; sprinkle with salt. Bake,
uncovered, in 375° oven for 30 minutes.

In medium saucepan, cook onion in 2 tablespoons butter till tender but not brown. Add
wine. Boil till wine is almost evaporated, 10 to
12 minutes. Blend in flour. Add milk, sour
cream, chicken extract, salt, pepper. Cook and
stir until mixture thickens and bubbles. Stir in
lemon juice. Strain. Reheat. Pour over capon.
Serve with wild rice. Makes 6 servings.

Roast Duck with Orange and Cointreau

2 3- to 4-pound ducks
2 stalks celery, cut in 2-inch pieces
1 small onion, quartered
2 carrots, quartered
1 orange, quartered
⅓ cup water
½ cup white wine
¼ cup dry sherry
1 orange
½ cup sugar
⅓ cup water
1 tablespoon lemon juice
1 tablespoon vinegar
1 tablespoon Cointreau orange liqueur
1 tablespoon cornstarch
⅛ teaspoon salt
   Dash pepper

Place ducks on rack in roasting pan. Stuff with celery, onion, carrot, and orange quarters. Roast, uncovered, in 375° oven for 1½ hours. Remove ducks to platter. Keep warm.

Skim fat from juices in pan. To pan add ⅓ cup water, wine, and sherry. Bring to boiling; boil until reduced to ¾ cup. In the meantime, squeeze orange, reserving juice. Scrape membrane and white portion from rinds of ½ the orange skin. Cut rind in very fine strips.

In a small saucepan, caramelize sugar; gradually stir in the remaining ⅓ cup water, reserved orange juice, lemon juice, and vinegar, stirring till caramel melts. Add orange rind strips and reduced wine mixture. Blend orange liqueur into cornstarch with salt and pepper. Add to sauce. Cook and stir until thickened and bubbly. Remove breast meat and legs from ducks; spoon sauce over. Makes 4 servings.

L'Escargot

Poulet à la Crème avec Truffe
(Chicken with Cream and Truffles)

- 2 2- to 2½-pound broiler-fryer chickens, cut up
- 4 tablespoons butter, melted
  Salt and pepper
- 2 cups whipping cream
- ½ cup Madeira wine
- ½ pound mushrooms, cut in large pieces (3 cups)
- ½ cup chopped truffle peelings
  Salt and pepper

Reserve bony parts of chicken for other uses. Place remaining pieces, skin side up, not touching, in greased 15x10x1-inch baking pan. Brush with melted butter. Season with salt and pepper. Bake in 375° oven about 1 hour or till done.

Transfer chicken to 12-inch skillet. Add cream, wine, mushrooms, and truffles. Bring to boil and boil gently on medium-high heat till cream thickens, about 18 minutes. Remove chicken to warm serving platter. Season sauce to taste with salt and pepper. Pour over chicken. Serve at once. Makes 4 servings.

THE CAFE BUDAPEST

Mushrooms Stuffed with Breast of Turkey

- ½ pound raw boned turkey or chicken breast*
- 2 1-inch slices French bread, torn (about 1½ cups)
- ½ medium onion, cut up

1 clove garlic
1 beaten egg
1 tablespoon water
3 tablespoons rendered chicken fat
¾ teaspoon salt
⅛ teaspoon pepper
1 pound large-size fresh mushrooms
2 tablespoons butter
½ medium onion, chopped (¼ cup)
2 tablespoons snipped parsley
¾ cup water
2 teaspoons lemon juice
¾ teaspoon salt
⅛ teaspoon pepper
½ cup light cream
¼ cup water
2 tablespoons all-purpose flour

Put turkey, bread, the ½ onion, and the garlic through fine blade of food grinder. Add egg, water, chicken fat, the ¾ teaspoon salt, and ⅛ teaspoon pepper; mix well. Remove stems from mushroom caps; slice enough stems to make 1½ cups. (Save remaining stems for another use.) Stuff mushroom caps with turkey mixture.

In large skillet, melt butter; add mushroom stems and the remaining onion; cook till tender. Remove from heat. Add parsley, the ¾ cup water, the lemon juice, and remaining salt and pepper to skillet. Place mushroom caps, stuffed side up, in skillet. Cover and cook over low heat 15 to 20 minutes or till turkey stuffing is done.

Remove mushrooms to serving dish; keep warm. Combine cream, remaining water, and flour; add to skillet mixture. Cook and stir till thickened and bubbly. Pour over mushrooms. Serve with rizi-bizi (boiled rice with peas) and a cranberry-orange sauce. Makes 4 servings.

*Raw boned chicken breast can be used if raw turkey breast is unavailable.

charley's crab
Troy, Michigan

Baked Stuffed Lobster Larry

 1 cup fresh mushrooms, sliced
¼ cup chopped onion
 2 tablespoons butter
 1 tablespoon all-purpose flour
¼ teaspoon salt
   Dash pepper
⅓ cup milk
 1 slightly beaten egg yolk
¼ cup fine dry bread crumbs
 6 ounces frozen crab meat or 1 7-ounce can
   crab meat, drained, flaked and cartilage
   removed
 2 live lobsters (about 1½ pounds each)
 4 tablespoons butter, melted
   Lemon wedges

In saucepan, cook mushrooms and onion in the 2 tablespoons butter; stir in flour, salt, and pepper. Add milk all at once; cook and stir till thickened and bubbly. Stir about half the hot mixture into beaten egg yolk; return all to saucepan. Cook and stir one minute more. Add bread crumbs, then carefully fold in crab meat. Set aside.

Plunge live lobsters into enough boiling salted water to cover. Return to boiling; reduce heat and simmer 10 minutes. Remove at once. Place on back. With sharp knife, cut in half lengthwise. Remove black vein that runs to tip of tail. Discard all organs in body section near head except red coral roe (females only) and brownish-green liver. Crack claws.

Spoon half of the stuffing mixture into body cavity of each lobster. Brush both lobsters with melted butter. Place in shallow baking pan. Bake, uncovered, in 475° oven for 10 to 12 minutes or till stuffing is heated through. Serve with lemon wedges and any remaining melted butter. Makes 2 servings.

Stuffed Lobster Tails à la Sea Gull

      4 lobster tails
      4 ounces shrimp, peeled and deveined
      4 ounces crab meat
      4 ounces scallops
    ⅔ cup sliced fresh mushrooms
      4 tablespoons butter
      2 tablespoons brandy
        White Sauce*
    ⅓ cup grated Parmesan cheese

Remove meat from lobster tails (reserve shells); cut meat into bite-size pieces. In skillet cook lobster, shrimp, crab, scallops, and mushrooms in butter till fish is done, about 5 minutes. Remove from heat; add brandy. Flame. When flame dies out, stir in White Sauce; heat through. Pile into lobster tail shells. Sprinkle with Parmesan cheese. Broil, 4 to 5 inches from heat, for 2 to 3 minutes, till lightly browned. Makes 4 servings.

 * **White Sauce:** In saucepan melt 2 tablespoons butter; blend in 3 tablespoons all-purpose flour, dash paprika, and dash ground red pepper. Stir in 1½ cups milk; cook and stir till thickened and bubbly. Stir in ¼ cup dry white wine.

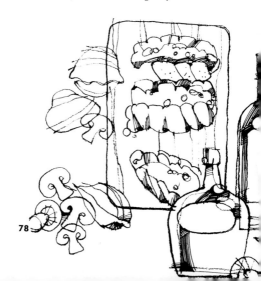

Lock Ober

Boston, Massachusetts

Baked Lobster Savannah

- 2 1½- to 2-pound live lobsters
- ½ cup sliced fresh mushrooms
- ¼ cup diced green pepper
- 3 tablespoons butter
- 2 tablespoons all-purpose flour
- 1 cup milk
- ¼ cup dry sherry
- 1 teaspoon paprika
- ½ teaspoon salt
- 2 tablespoons diced pimiento
- ¼ cup shredded sharp American cheese
     (1 ounce)
- ¼ cup soft bread crumbs

Plunge live lobsters into enough boiling, salted water to cover. Bring to boiling; reduce heat and simmer till done, 20 minutes. Remove and cool. Cut off claws, legs, and head. Hold lobster top side up; with kitchen shears, cut an oval opening in top of shell from base of head to tail. Discard organs. Remove all meat from body and claws; cut meat into cubes.

In saucepan, cook mushrooms and green pepper in butter till tender. Blend in flour; add milk. Cook and stir till thickened and bubbly. Add sherry, paprika, and salt; cook and stir 2 minutes more. Remove from heat. Stir in lobster meat and pimiento. Pile into lobster shells. Place on baking sheet. Sprinkle with mixture of cheese and bread crumbs. Bake in 375° oven for 15 minutes. Makes 2 servings.

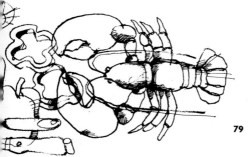

79

Crabe Wallis

- 5 ounces mushrooms, quartered (1½ cups)
- 2 chopped shallots (1 tablespoon)
- 4 tablespoons butter
- 5 tablespoons all-purpose flour
    Dash dried thyme, crushed
- 1 cup light cream
- ½ cup dry white wine
    Salt
    White pepper
    Cayenne
- 8 ounces fresh crab meat *or* frozen crab
    meat, thawed
    Grated Parmesan cheese

In large saucepan, cook mushrooms and shallots in butter till tender but not brown. Blend in flour and thyme. Stir in cream; cook and stir till thickened and bubbly. Add wine. Season to taste with salt, pepper, and cayenne. Stir in crab meat.

Spoon into individual shells or ramekins. Sprinkle with Parmesan cheese. Bake in 400° oven for about 15 minutes, till crab is done and top is lightly browned. Makes 6 servings.

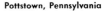

Gretna, Louisiana

Lump Crab Meat and Crayfish Cardinal

- 2 chopped shallots (1 tablespoon)
- 1 tablespoon butter
- ¼ cup dry white wine
- ¼ cup tomato sauce

4 tablespoons butter
   4 tablespoons all-purpose flour
½ teaspoon salt
1¼ cups milk
   8 ounces lump crab meat (if frozen, thaw)
   1 pound shrimp, peeled and deveined
     Salt
     Cayenne
     Hot cooked rice

In saucepan, cook shallots in the 1 tablespoon butter till tender but not brown. Add wine and tomato sauce; simmer, uncovered, till reduced to ¼ cup, about 5 minutes.

Meanwhile, in another saucepan, melt remaining 4 tablespoons butter; blend in flour and ½ teaspoon salt. Add milk, all at once; cook and stir till thickened and bubbly. Add to tomato sauce mixture. Return to boil; stir in crab meat and shrimp. Cook and stir gently till fish is heated through, about 5 minutes. Season to taste with salt and cayenne. Serve with rice. Makes 4 servings.

GAGE&TOLLNER   Brooklyn, New York

Bay Scallops Newburg

   2 tablespoons butter
   2 tablespoons all-purpose flour
¼ teaspoon salt
⅛ teaspoon paprika
   1 cup milk
   3 tablespoons dry sherry
   1 cup bay scallops (7 ounces)
     Toast points

In small saucepan, melt butter. Add flour, salt, and paprika. Stir in milk and cook, stirring constantly till mixture thickens and bubbles. Add the sherry. Add the bay scallops and cook gently in sauce for 5 minutes. Serve on toast points. Makes 2 servings.

Shrimp Creole

- 16 ounces fresh or frozen shrimp, thawed, peeled, and deveined
- ¼ cup chopped celery
- ¼ cup chopped onion
- 2 tablespoons finely chopped salt pork
- 1 16-ounce can whole tomatoes, cut up
- ¼ cup chili sauce
- 2 teaspoons sugar
- ½ teaspoon dried thyme
- ½ teaspoon beef flavored gravy base
- 1 clove garlic, minced
  Salt and pepper
  Hot cooked rice

Cook shrimp in boiling salted water 1 to 3 minutes or till done. Drain and set aside. In saucepan, cook celery, onion, and salt pork till celery is tender, about 5 minutes. Add tomatoes, chili sauce, sugar, thyme, gravy base, and garlic. Season to taste with salt and pepper. Cover and simmer 30 minutes. Add shrimp; heat through. Serve with rice. Makes 4 servings.

Antolotti's

New York, New York

Shrimp Antolotti

- 36 raw shrimp
- 2 well-beaten eggs
- 1 tablespoon cornstarch
- 1 tablespoon lemon juice
- 1 tablespoon all-purpose flour
  - Oil for deep frying
- 3 tablespoons all-purpose flour
- 4 tablespoons butter, melted
- ½ cup dry white wine
- ½ cup condensed chicken broth
- ¼ cup clam juice
- 1 tablespoon lemon juice
- ½ teaspoon salt
  - Dash pepper
  - Snipped parsley

Shell and devein shrimp. With tip of sharp knife, slit down back to butterfly the shrimp. Rinse and dry well. In small bowl, combine eggs, cornstarch, and lemon juice. Dip shrimp into the 1 tablespoon flour; shake off excess, then dip in egg batter. Fry a few at a time in hot oil (375°) till browned, about 3 minutes. Dry on paper toweling.

In medium saucepan, blend the 3 tablespoons flour and melted butter. Add wine, chicken broth, and clam juice. Cook and stir till thickened. Stir in lemon juice, salt, and pepper. Fold in shrimp. Turn into serving casserole; top with parsley. Makes 4 servings.

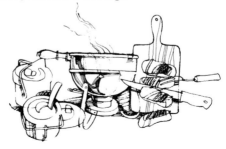

Scampi Ondine

- 2 medium tomatoes, peeled and chopped (1⅓ cups)
- 2 tablespoons olive oil
- 2 bay leaves
- 2 cloves garlic
- ½ teaspoon salt
- ⅛ teaspoon pepper
- 20 fresh or frozen scampi or jumbo shrimp, thawed (1½ pounds)
- ¼ cup milk
- ⅓ cup all-purpose flour
  Salt
- ¾ cup olive oil
- 3 tablespoons butter
- 2 cloves garlic, finely chopped
- 2 tablespoons lemon juice
  Snipped parsley

In small saucepan, combine chopped tomatoes, the 2 tablespoons olive oil, bay leaves, the 2 garlic cloves, salt, and pepper. Bring to boil; reduce heat. Cover and simmer till tomatoes are tender, about 5 minutes. Remove garlic and bay leaf. Strain fresh-cooked (or 8 ounces canned stewed) tomatoes and set pulp aside.

Peel, devein, and butterfly scampi. Dip scampi in milk, then in flour, shaking off excess flour. Sprinkle scampi lightly with salt. In large skillet, heat remaining olive oil. Add about half the scampi at a time. Cook, uncovered, over medium heat till scampi are done, about 3 minutes per side. Drain on paper toweling.

In another saucepan, melt butter; cook chopped garlic in butter till tender. Add tomato pulp and lemon juice; mix well. Drain olive oil from scampi pan. Pour tomato sauce over scampi. Sprinkle with parsley. Mix gently and serve immediately. Makes 4 servings.

Coquilles St. Jacques Petits Legumes
(Scallops and Vegetables in Shells)

- ⅔ cup clam juice
- ⅔ cup dry white wine
- ¼ cup chopped shallots
- 1 pound scallops
- 1 cup milk
- 1 cup sliced fresh mushrooms
- ½ cup thinly sliced carrot strips
- ½ cup thinly sliced celery strips
- 6 cups torn fresh spinach (8 ounces)
- 2 tablespoons butter
  Salt and pepper
- ½ cup whipping cream
- 2 tablespoons butter
- 2 teaspoons lemon juice

In saucepan, combine clam juice, wine, and shallots; boil hard to reduce to ⅔ cup. Set aside. Bring scallops, milk, salt, and pepper to boil; reduce heat. Cover and simmer till scallops are done, about 4 minutes. Drain. (Use poaching liquid for other cooking purposes, if desired.)

Simmer mushrooms, carrots, and celery, covered, in small amount boiling salted water till tender, about 3 minutes. Drain and set aside.

In large covered skillet, cook spinach in 2 tablespoons butter just till limp, about 1 to 2 minutes. Sprinkle lightly with salt and pepper. Spoon spinach into 4 large coquille shells (or individual casseroles); top with scallops, then with mushroom mixture.

Bake in 350° oven for 10 minutes or till heated through. Meanwhile, combine clam-wine mixture and whipping cream. Boil, uncovered, till mixture thickens, stirring occasionally (about 8 minutes). Add 2 tablespoons butter and lemon juice. Spoon over baked scallops. Makes 4 main dish servings.

Doros

San Francisco, California

Veal Scaloppine à la Doros

1½	pounds veal sirloin
⅓	cup all-purpose flour
¾	teaspoon salt
⅛	teaspoon pepper
12	eggplant slices, ½ inch thick
4	tablespoons cooking oil
2	tablespoons butter
1	pound sliced fresh mushrooms
4	tablespoons butter
1	tablespoon shallots, chopped
½	cup dry sauterne
¾	cup condensed beef broth
2	tablespoons all-purpose flour
2	tablespoons butter
¼	cup chopped parsley

Cut meat into 12 even pieces; pound till thin (about ⅛ inch thick). Combine ⅓ cup flour, salt, and pepper. Dip veal pieces to coat slightly. Set aside.

In skillet, cook eggplant in hot oil for 2 to 3 minutes per side or till tender and brown. Drain. Keep warm in slow oven. In same skillet melt the 2 tablespoons butter; stir in mushrooms. Cover and cook 8 to 10 minutes, stirring occasionally. Meanwhile, in a 12-inch skillet melt 2 tablespoons butter. Quickly brown about ½ of the veal at a time, about 1½ minutes per side. Melt 2 tablespoons more butter for second half of veal. Remove to platter and keep warm.

To same pan add shallots and wine; simmer 3 minutes. Blend beef broth and 2 tablespoons flour; stir into wine mixture. Cook and stir till thickened and bubbly. Add 2 tablespoons butter; stir to melt. Arrange eggplant and veal overlapping atop the mushrooms on a platter. Pour sauce over all. Sprinkle with parsley. Makes 4 servings.

L'ETOILE

San Francisco, California

L'Escalopine de Veau au Champagne
(Veal Scaloppine with Champagne)

- ¼ cup all-purpose flour
- ½ teaspoon salt
- ⅛ teaspoon pepper
- 1 pound scaloppine of veal (12 slices)
- 3 tablespoons butter
- 1 cup Champagne
- 1 cup sliced mushrooms
- 1 cup whipping cream
- 2 tablespoons Cognac
- Salt
- White pepper

Stir together flour, ½ teaspoon salt, and ⅛ teaspoon pepper. Dip veal in flour mixture, coating both sides. Melt butter in large skillet. Brown half of the veal at a time on both sides, about 1 to 1½ minutes per side. Transfer to platter and keep warm. Stir Champagne into skillet; add mushrooms and cream. Boil till thickened, about 10 to 12 minutes. Stir in Cognac and season with salt and pepper. Pour over veal and serve. Makes 4 servings.

Blanquette de Veau

(White Ragout of Veal)

        2 whole cloves
        1 medium onion
    2½ pounds veal, cut in 1-inch cubes
        1 pound small onions (12 to 14)
        3 cups water
        1 teaspoon salt
      ¼ teaspoon pepper
      ½ teaspoon dried thyme, crushed
      12 mushroom caps
        2 tablespoons butter
        1 tablespoon lemon juice
            Dash salt
    1½ cups chicken broth
        4 tablespoons butter
      ¼ cup all-purpose flour
        2 beaten egg yolks
      ½ cup whipping cream

Stick cloves into medium onion. Place in large saucepan along with veal, small onions, 3 cups water, 1 teaspoon salt, pepper, and thyme. Cover and simmer 40 to 45 minutes or till meat is tender. Drain. Set meat aside.

Return liquid to pan; boil, uncovered, 5 minutes or until reduced to 1 cup liquid. Meanwhile in covered skillet cook mushroom caps in 2 tablespoons butter, lemon juice, and salt for 5 minutes. Drain, reserving juices. Combine mushroom juices and reduced pan juices; add chicken broth to make 2½ cups.

In the saucepan, melt 4 tablespoons butter; blend in flour. Add stock mixture. Cook and stir till mixture thickens and boils. Combine egg yolks and cream; stir into thickened mixture. Add mushrooms, onion, and veal. Heat through but do not boil. Makes 6 servings.

The Lemon Tree

Lancaster, Pennsylvania

Veau à la Crème aux Chataigne
(Veal Chataigne with Green Noodles in Cream)

    2   pounds veal, cut in 1-inch cubes
    2   to 3 tablespoons butter
  1/3   cup chopped onion
    1   clove garlic, minced
1 1/2   teaspoons salt
  1/4   teaspoon pepper
  1/4   cup all-purpose flour
  1/2   cup brandy
  3/4   cup chicken broth
    8   ounces fresh mushrooms, sliced (3 cups)
    1   8-ounce can water chestnuts, drained and
          sliced (1 cup)
    1   cup heavy cream
        Hot cooked green spinach noodles

In ovenproof skillet, brown veal in hot butter. Add onion, garlic, salt, and pepper. Cook and stir till onion is tender, about 3 minutes. Blend in flour. Add brandy, ignite. When flame has subsided, add broth. Cover and bake in 400° oven for 30 minutes or till meat is tender.

Remove from oven. Add mushrooms, water chestnuts, and cream. Stir till blended. Simmer 5 minutes. Serve over green noodles. Garnish with parsley. Makes 6 servings.

Vitello Tartufatto
(Veal Tartufatto)

  1 pound veal, cut in 12 thin slices
     (about ⅛ inch thick)
     Salt
     Pepper
  ¼ cup all-purpose flour
  6 tablespoons clarified butter
  1 tablespoon chopped shallots
  ½ cup Madeira wine
  2 tablespoons all-purpose flour
  ¼ cup whipping cream
  ¾ cup beef broth

Sprinkle veal with salt and pepper; dip in the ¼ cup flour. In large skillet, heat 4 tablespoons of the butter; when hot, add veal, half at a time, and brown quickly on both sides. Arrange on serving platter; keep warm.

In same skillet, cook shallots in the remaining butter. Remove from heat; allow pan to cool slightly. Add Madeira; flame. When flame is extinguished, blend 2 tablespoons flour, cream, and broth. Add to skillet. Cook and stir till thickened. Strain. Serve over veal slices. Sprinkle with chopped truffles, if desired. Makes 6 servings.

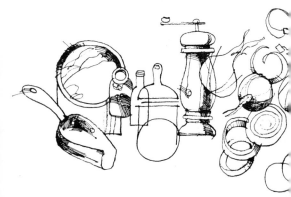

Swiss Hütte

Côte de Veau Normande
(Veal Chops with Mushrooms and Cream)

- 4 veal chops, ¾ inch thick
  (about 2 pounds)
- 1 tablespoon cooking oil
  Salt
  Pepper
- 2 tablespoons butter
- 2 tablespoons minced shallots
- ½ cup dry white wine
- ½ cup chicken broth
- 1 cup sliced fresh mushrooms
- 2 tablespoons butter
- ¼ cup apple brandy
- ½ cup whipping cream
- 2 teaspoons arrowroot
- ¼ teaspoon salt
- ⅛ teaspoon pepper

In ovenproof skillet, brown chops in hot oil 5 minutes per side. Season with salt and pepper. Remove and set aside. Pour off fat. To skillet add 2 tablespoons butter and shallots; cook till tender but not brown. Add white wine and chicken broth. Boil, scraping pan, till reduced to ½ cup. Return chops to skillet; spoon juices over. Cover; bake in 400° oven for 15 minutes.

Meanwhile in small saucepan, cook mushrooms in 2 tablespoons butter for 2 minutes. Remove chops to platter. Keep warm. To skillet, add brandy; flame. After flame subsides blend cream into arrowroot. Add to skillet; cook and stir till mixture thickens. Add ¼ teaspoon salt, ⅛ teaspoon pepper, and mushrooms. Spoon over chops and serve. Makes 4 servings.

Atlanta, Georgia

Crabacado Salad

- ½ cup mayonnaise
- ½ cup dairy sour cream
- 1 tablespoon Dijon-style mustard
- 1 teaspoon lemon juice
- 1 teaspoon Worcestershire sauce
- ¼ cup minced celery
- ¼ cup minced, drained capers
- 1 hard-cooked egg, minced
- 2 tablespoons minced, drained pimiento
- 1 tablespoon minced parsley
- 1 head leaf lettuce
- 2 chilled ripe avocados, halved, seeded, and peeled
- 2 6-ounce packages crab meat, drained
- 4 chilled tomatoes, peeled
- 4 chilled artichoke hearts, drained
- 4 chilled hard-cooked eggs
- 16 chilled, whole, pitted black olives

In mixing bowl, blend together mayonnaise, sour cream, mustard, lemon juice, and Worcestershire. Stir in celery, capers, minced egg, pimiento, and parsley. Chill.

Arrange leaf lettuce on four salad plates. Place one avocado half on each plate. Reserve a little crab for garnish; divide remaining between the four avocado halves. Spoon a fourth of the dressing over each avocado. Place one piece of reserved crab on top. Sprinkle each salad lightly with paprika.

Cut each tomato in half lengthwise. Place one-half of the tomato on each end of the avocado. Cut each artichoke heart in half lengthwise, starting at the stem end, and place on each side of the filled avocado. Cut each hard-cooked egg in quarter wedges and place on each corner of the salad platter. Place one whole black olive alongside each quarter of egg. Serve immediately. Makes 4 servings.

La Vieille Varsovie

Dallas, Texas

The Old Warsaw Salad

- ¾ cup salad oil
- ¼ cup red wine vinegar
- 2 egg yolks
- 1 tablespoon chopped parsley
- 2 teaspoons chopped onion
- 1 small clove garlic, minced
- 1 teaspoon chopped shallots
- 2 teaspoons Dijon-style mustard
- ⅛ teaspoon dried tarragon, crushed
  Dash pepper
  Few drops Worcestershire sauce
- 1½ cups fresh mushrooms, sliced (4 ounces)

  . . .

- 1 medium head Boston lettuce (4 cups torn)
- 4 cups fresh spinach, stems removed
- ½ head romaine (6 cups torn)
- 2 French endive (6 ounces)
- 1 14-ounce can hearts of palm, drained and cut in bite-size pieces
- 1 14-ounce can artichoke hearts, drained and quartered
- 1 avocado, seeded, peeled, and sliced lengthwise
- 2 tablespoons coarsely chopped walnuts

Dressing: In large jar, combine oil, vinegar, egg yolks, parsley, onion, garlic, shallots, mustard, tarragon, pepper, and Worcestershire. Cover and shake vigorously. Add mushrooms.

Salad: Wash and pat dry the lettuce, spinach, romaine, and endive. Place in salad bowl. Add hearts of palm, artichoke hearts, and avocado slices; sprinkle walnuts atop. Toss with dressing. Makes 8 servings.

Madame Wu's Shredded Chicken Salad

  2 whole chicken breasts
     Oil for deep frying
  8 squares wonton dough, cut in ⅛-inch strips
  2 ounces (about 2 cups) rice noodles
     (rice sticks)
¼ cup soy sauce
  1 tablespoon prepared mustard
  1 teaspoon sesame oil
  1 teaspoon Five Spice Powder
½ cup sliced green onion
¼ cup chopped toasted almonds
     Shredded lettuce

Cook chicken breasts, covered, in boiling, salted water for 20 minutes, or till tender. Drain well; dry with paper toweling. Remove skin. Place one at a time in 365° (hot) oil for 3 to 4 minutes, till crisp and golden. Drain on paper toweling. Remove meat from bones; cut into strips.

In same oil, fry wonton strips, one-fourth at a time, till golden, about 30 seconds. Next fry rice noodles, one-fourth at a time. Remove rice noodles as soon as they puff, so that they do not become fat-soaked. Drain.

In large bowl, combine soy sauce, mustard, sesame oil, and spice powder. Add chicken and onion; toss to coat well. Cover and chill. Just before serving, add rice noodles, wontons, and almonds; toss gently. Pile salad on bed of shredded lettuce. Makes 4 servings.

Canlis' Salad

- 2 tablespoons olive oil
  Salt
- 1 clove garlic
- 2 tomatoes, peeled and cut in wedges
- 2 heads romaine, cut in 1-inch strips
- 1 pound bacon, crisp-cooked and crumbled fine
- ½ cup grated Romano cheese
- ¼ cup sliced green onion
- ⅓ cup olive oil
- ⅓ cup lemon juice
- ½ teaspoon fresh-ground pepper
- ¼ teaspoon chopped fresh mint
- ¼ teaspoon dried oregano, crushed
- 1 coddled egg
- 1 cup croutons

Into a large salad bowl, pour 2 tablespoons of olive oil; sprinkle with a little salt and rub with the clove of garlic. Remove garlic and discard. To the bowl, add the tomatoes, romaine, bacon, cheese, and green onions.

In small bowl, combine the ⅓ cup oil, lemon juice, pepper, mint, oregano, and egg for dressing; beat well. Pour over salad and toss lightly. Add croutons. Makes 8 servings.

La Louisiane

deGaulle or Cresson Salad Dressing

¼ bunch watercress (2 cups with stems)
2 tablespoons lemon juice
2 cloves garlic, peeled and sliced
   Dash salt
   Dash pepper
1 cup mayonnaise

Rinse and remove leaves of watercress from stems. In blender container, place lemon juice, garlic, watercress, salt, and pepper. Blend well. Remove from container. Stir into mayonnaise; cover and chill. Serve with salads or cold seafood. Makes 1¼ cups.

Karl Ratzsch's

Milwaukee, Wisconsin

Walnut Nut Roll

- 1 package active dry yeast
- 1 tablespoon sugar
- 2 tablespoons warm water
- 2 cups all-purpose flour
- 1 tablespoon sugar
- ¼ teaspoon salt
- 4 tablespoons butter
- 2 beaten egg yolks
- ½ cup dairy sour cream
- ½ teaspoon finely shredded lemon peel
- 1 cup walnuts, ground
- ⅓ cup sugar
- ¼ cup raisins
- 1 tablespoon lemon juice
- 1 tablespoon water
- 2 beaten egg whites

Soften yeast and 1 tablespoon of the sugar in the 2 tablespoons water; set aside. In mixing bowl, combine flour, remaining 1 tablespoon sugar, and salt. Cut in butter till mixture resembles fine crumbs. Blend in yeast mixture, egg yolks, sour cream, and lemon peel to make a soft dough. Cover; let rise in warm place for 2 hours or till double.

Punch down. Roll out on lightly floured surface to a 12x14-inch rectangle. Combine ground walnuts, ⅓ cup sugar, and raisins. Blend in lemon juice and 1 tablespoon water. Spread over dough. Roll up jelly-roll fashion beginning with long side. Place on greased baking sheet. Let rise in warm place 1 hour or till double. Brush with beaten egg white. Bake in 350° oven for 25 to 30 minutes. Makes 1 nut roll.

french cafe

Gâteau Moelleux d'Asperges
(Baked Asparagus Custards)

- 2 pounds fresh green asparagus
- 2 eggs
- 1 egg yolk
- 1 teaspoon salt
- ¼ teaspoon ground nutmeg
  Dash pepper
- 1 10½-ounce can white asparagus spears, drained
- ¼ cup chicken broth
- ¼ cup light cream
- ¼ teaspoon salt
  Dash ground pepper
- ½ medium tomato, peeled, seeded, and diced
- 1 tablespoon snipped parsley

Clean fresh asparagus; break off and discard tough parts. Cook asparagus in boiling, salted water for 10 to 15 minutes, till tender. Drain well. Cut off 12 tips; set aside for garnish. Chop remaining asparagus; purée in blender container (should have 2 cups purée).

In mixing bowl, beat eggs, egg yolk, the 1 teaspoon salt, nutmeg, and pepper. Stir in asparagus purée. Turn into 4 lightly greased 6-ounce custard cups. Place in large baking pan; add boiling water to pan to depth of 1 inch. Bake in 400° oven for 30 minutes, till set.

Meanwhile, place canned asparagus, chicken broth, cream, remaining salt, and pepper in blender container. Blend till smooth. Turn into a small saucepan; heat through. Season to taste. Unmold custards onto serving plates. Spoon sauce around them. Garnish with chopped tomato, parsley, and asparagus tips reheated in small amount boiling water. Makes 4 servings.

Maisonette

Epinards au Beurre ou à la Crème
(Creamed Spinach)

- 2 pounds leaf spinach
- ⅓ cup unsalted butter
  - Salt
  - Pepper
  - Nutmeg
- 1½ cups whipping cream
- 8 Timbales or patty shells

Parboil the spinach in plenty of boiling salted water; cool. Press out all the water from spinach; chop the spinach. In saucepan, combine the chopped spinach with the butter. Dry over high heat. Season to taste with pepper and nutmeg. Add the cream and cook for 10 minutes. Spoon into a timbale when ready to serve and sprinkle with a few drops of cream. Makes 8 servings.

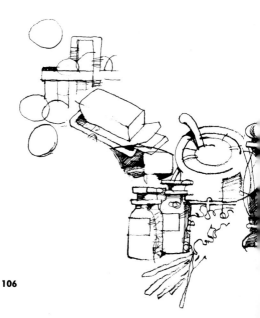

PETITE MARMITE

Potatoes Amandine

- 2 baking potatoes
- 4 tablespoons butter
- ½ cup boiling water
- ½ cup all-purpose flour
- 2 eggs
- ½ teaspoon salt
- Dash pepper
- ¼ teaspoon ground nutmeg
- ¼ cup all-purpose flour
- 1 beaten egg
- 1 cup sliced almonds, chopped
- Oil for deep frying

Bake potatoes in 425° oven for 1 hour, till tender. Melt butter in ½ cup boiling water. Add ½ cup flour all at once; stir vigorously. Cook and stir till mixture forms a ball that doesn't separate. Remove from heat; cool slightly. Add 2 eggs, one at a time, beating after each till smooth.

Peel the hot potatoes; mash. Season with salt and pepper; add nutmeg. Add potatoes to cooked flour mixture; mix well. Chill. Using 1 rounded tablespoon dough, shape into sixteen 2-inch logs. Dip in additional ¼ cup flour, then in beaten egg. Roll in almonds. Heat ½ inch oil in 10-inch skillet. Fry half of the rolls at a time about 2 minutes, turning once. Makes 8 servings.

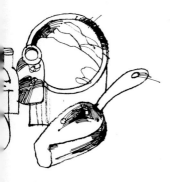

GAY LORD

New York, New York

Chhole Masala
(Chickpeas)

    8 ounces (1¼ cups) dried chickpeas (garbanzo beans)

    9 cups water

    1 tablespoon salt

    2 tablespoons cooking oil

    1 medium onion, sliced and separated into rings (about 1½ cups)

    2 hot green peppers, seeded, rinsed, and finely chopped (2 tablespoons)

    ½ medium tomato, peeled and chopped

    ½ teaspoon ground cinnamon

    ¼ teaspoon ground cloves

    ¼ teaspoon ground cumin

    ¼ teaspoon cayenne

    ¼ teaspoon turmeric

    Dash pepper

    1 medium potato, diced (1 cup)

 1½ teaspoons salt

    ⅛ teaspoon pepper

    1 sprig fresh coriander leaves, chopped

Wash chickpeas. In large kettle, combine chickpeas and water. Soak overnight. To kettle add the 1 tablespoon salt; cover and boil till tender, about 1½ hours. Do not drain.

In small saucepan, heat oil; add onion, green pepper, tomato, and spices. Cover and simmer 15 minutes. Add to the chickpeas along with potato, 1½ teaspoons salt, pepper, and coriander. Bring to boiling; reduce heat and simmer 10 minutes. Makes 6 servings.

Blue Fox

San Francisco, California

Tomato Timbale

    8 tomatoes, peeled
      Salt
    1 teaspoon chopped shallots
    2 tablespoons butter
    2 tablespoons all-purpose flour
  ½ cup sherry
  ½ cup chicken broth
    1 10-ounce package chopped broccoli,
      cooked and drained
  ¼ teaspoon dried basil
  ⅛ teaspoon ground nutmeg
  ⅛ teaspoon salt
      Dash pepper
      Hollandaise Sauce (optional — page 2)

Cut about ¼ inch off tops of tomatoes; scoop out centers and turn shells over to drain. Sprinkle shells with salt. Set aside.

In small saucepan, cook shallots in butter till tender but not brown; blend in flour. Add sherry and chicken broth. Cook and stir till thickened and bubbly. Cook 2 minutes more. Stir in broccoli, basil, nutmeg, salt, and pepper.

Pile mixture into shells. Place stuffed tomatoes in ½-cup fluted salad molds. Arrange molds in 15x10x1-inch baking pan. Bake in 350° oven 25 to 30 minutes. To serve, invert mold onto serving plates and garnish with a little Hollandaise Sauce, if desired. Makes 8 servings.

Perditas

St. Honoré Pie

- 1 envelope unflavored gelatin
- ¼ cup granulated sugar
- 1½ cups milk
- 3 slightly beaten egg yolks
- ⅛ teaspoon salt
- 2 tablespoons brandy or rum
- 1 teaspoon vanilla
- 1 cup soft macaroon crumbs
- ½ cup pecans, finely chopped *or* chestnuts, finely chopped
- ⅓ cup raisins, chopped
- 2 tablespoons almonds, ground
- 3 egg whites
- ¼ cup granulated sugar
- 1 baked 9-inch pastry shell
- 1 cup fresh strawberries
- 1 cup whipping cream
  Pecan halves

In saucepan, combine gelatin and ¼ cup sugar; add milk, egg yolks, and salt. Cook and stir till mixture is slightly thickened and gelatin is dissolved. Stir in brandy and vanilla. Chill till partially set. Stir in macaroon crumbs, ½ cup pecans, raisins and almonds.

In mixer bowl, beat egg whites to soft peaks; gradually add remaining ¼ cup sugar beating to stiff peaks. Fold into gelatin mixture. Turn into prepared pastry shell. Chill till set.

Slice strawberries and arrange atop pie. Whip cream to soft peaks. Spoon atop pie. Garnish with pecan halves. Makes 6 servings.

Grasshopper Pie

- 1 tablespoon unflavored gelatin
- ¼ cup cold water
- ½ cup sugar
- 2 tablespoons cornstarch
- 2 cups milk
- 4 slightly beaten egg yolks
- 1 1-ounce square unsweetened chocolate, melted
- 1 teaspoon vanilla
- 1 9-inch chocolate cookie crust
- ¼ cup crème de menthe
- ¼ cup white crème de cacao
- 4 egg whites
- ¼ cup sugar
  Whipped cream
  Shaved semisweet chocolate

Soften gelatin in water. In 2-quart saucepan, combine the ½ cup sugar and cornstarch. Stir in milk and egg yolks. Cook and stir until mixture thickens and bubbles. Remove 1 cup of custard mixture; stir in chocolate and vanilla. Spread evenly in crust.

Stir softened gelatin into remaining custard. Cool. Add crème de menthe and crème de cacao. Chill till partially set. Beat egg whites to soft peaks. Add ¼ cup sugar gradually beating to stiff peaks. Fold in gelatin mixture. Pile on top of chocolate layer in crust. Chill 4 to 6 hours. Garnish with whipped cream and shaved chocolate. Makes 8 servings.

Praline Ice Cream Pie

- ½ cup packed brown sugar
- ½ cup whipping cream
- 2 tablespoons butter
- 1 cup chopped pecans
- 1 teaspoon vanilla
- 1½ quarts vanilla ice cream
- 1 baked 9-inch pastry shell
- 3 egg whites
- ½ teaspoon vanilla
- ¼ teaspoon cream of tartar
- ⅓ cup granulated sugar
- Rum Sauce*

In medium skillet, heat and stir brown sugar over medium-low heat just till sugar melts, about 10 to 12 minutes. Gradually blend in cream; cook 2 to 3 minutes more, or till smooth. Remove from heat; stir in butter, pecans, and 1 teaspoon vanilla. Cool.

Stir ice cream just to soften. Quickly fold in praline mixture. Turn into pastry shell. Freeze. Just before serving, beat egg whites, the ½ teaspoon vanilla, and the cream of tartar to soft peaks. Gradually add granulated sugar, beating to stiff peaks. Spread meringue atop ice cream, sealing to edge. Bake in 475° oven for 4 to 5 minutes, or till lightly browned. Serve immediately with Rum Sauce.

*Rum Sauce: In small saucepan combine 2 beaten egg yolks, ½ teaspoon grated lemon peel, ¼ cup lemon juice, ¼ cup sugar, and 4 tablespoons butter. Cook and stir till thickened. Stir in 3 tablespoons light rum. Makes about 1 cup.

Riz a L'Impératrice
(Rice Empress Style)

⅓ cup candied fruits and peels
⅓ cup Kirsch (cherry brandy)
1 envelope unflavored gelatin
¼ cup water
2 cups milk
¼ cup sugar
3 tablespoons uncooked rice
¼ teaspoon salt
1 2-inch piece vanilla bean
2 beaten eggs
1 cup whipping cream, whipped

. . .

1 cup milk
2 tablespoons sugar
1 2-inch piece vanilla bean
2 beaten egg yolks
2 tablespoons Kirsch (cherry brandy)

Combine candied fruit and peel and ⅓ cup Kirsch; let soak 3 hours. Soften gelatin in water. In saucepan, combine 2 cups milk, ¼ cup sugar, rice, ¼ teaspoon salt, and a 2-inch piece of vanilla bean. Cook and stir until mixture bubbles. Reduce heat. Cover and simmer till rice is tender, about 30 minutes, stirring occasionally.

Stir in softened gelatin. Gradually stir about half of the rice mixture into eggs. Return to saucepan; cook and stir till mixture bubbles. Remove vanilla bean. Stir in soaked fruit and Kirsch. Chill till partially set. Fold in whipped cream. Turn into 5-cup mold. Chill 4 to 6 hours or overnight. Serve with Sauce au Kirsch. Makes 6 servings.

Sauce au Kirsch: In small saucepan, combine 1 cup milk, 2 tablespoons sugar, dash salt, and remaining vanilla bean. Over low heat, stir until milk is hot; remove vanilla bean. Gradually stir about half the milk into yolks. Return all to saucepan; cook and stir till mixture coats a metal spoon. Add 2 tablespoons Kirsch. Pour into a bowl. Cool, then chill.

Fried Cream with Rum

- ⅓ cup sugar
- ⅓ cup all-purpose flour
- ⅛ teaspoon salt
- 1⅓ cups milk
- 1 slightly beaten egg
- 2 slightly beaten egg yolks
- 2 teaspoons vanilla
- 1 egg
- 1 tablespoon water
- ¾ cup fine bread crumbs
  Oil for deep frying
- 3 tablespoons rum

Line bottom and sides of 9x5x3-inch pan with foil. In saucepan, combine sugar, flour, and salt. Stir in milk. Add slightly beaten egg and egg yolks. Cook and stir until thickened and bubbly, about 10 minutes. Remove from heat; add vanilla. Spread pudding evenly in foil-lined pan. Cool; cover and chill thoroughly, several hours or overnight. Turn out onto waxed paper. Remove foil and cut into 4 pieces lengthwise and 9 crosswise.

Beat remaining egg and water. Dip cream pieces into egg then in bread crumbs. Chill, uncovered, about 1 hour. Fry in hot oil (365°) about 1 minute or until browned. Lift from oil with slotted spoon. Place in heat-proof serving dish; keep warm until all have been fried. Sprinkle with sugar. Flame heated rum; pour over fried cream. Serve immediately in individual dishes. Makes 6 servings.

Stonehenge Apple Fritters

- 4 apples, peeled and cored
  All-purpose flour
- ¾ cup all-purpose flour
- ½ teaspoon paprika
- ¼ teaspoon salt
  Dash pepper
- ¾ cup beer
  Oil for deep frying
- ¼ cup sugar
- ¼ teaspoon ground cinnamon

. . .

- 1½ tablespoons sugar
- 1½ teaspoons cornstarch
- 1 cup milk
- 1 beaten egg
- ¼ teaspoon vanilla
- 2 tablespoons Kirschwasser
- ¼ cup whipping cream, whipped

Slice apples into ½-inch wedges; coat lightly with flour. In bowl, combine the ¾ cup flour, paprika, salt, and pepper. Add beer; beat smooth. Dip apples into batter. Fry in hot oil (375°) until golden, about 1 minute per side. Drain. Roll in ¼ cup sugar and cinnamon. Spoon about ¼ cup Bavarian Sauce into dish; arrange fritters in sauce. Serve immediately. Makes 4 to 6 servings.

Bavarian Sauce: In 1-quart saucepan, mix sugar and cornstarch. Stir in milk and egg. Cook and stir over medium-high heat, stirring constantly, for about 9 minutes, till mixture thickens and bubbles. Add vanilla. Cool. Stir in Kirschwasser. Fold in whipped cream. Chill. Makes 1½ cups.

Zabaglione

½ cup Marsala wine
3 tablespoons sugar
4 egg yolks
  Dash salt
  Few drops vanilla
  Strawberries
  Cinnamon

In the top of a double boiler, combine wine and sugar. Place over simmering water (upper pan should not touch water). Add egg yolks and salt. Using wire whisk, beat till mixture thickens and mounds, about 8 minutes. Beat in vanilla. Serve in a tall glass over strawberries. Sprinkle lightly with cinnamon. Serve with wafers if desired. Makes 4 servings.

Anthony's
San Diego, California

Strawberries à la San Diego

½ cup dairy sour cream
½ cup lo-cal cream
1 tablespoon brown sugar
1 tablespoon rum
1 tablespoon orange liqueur
20 large strawberries, with stems

In small bowl, combine all ingredients except strawberries till blended. Serve dip in four individual dishes. Arrange strawberries on a larger bowl of crushed ice. Dip stemmed berries into cream mixture. Makes 4 servings.

Brennan's

Bananas Foster

- 4 tablespoons butter
- ¼ cup packed brown sugar
- ½ teaspoon ground cinnamon
- 2 tablespoons banana liqueur
- 4 medium-size firm bananas, halved lengthwise and crosswise
- ¼ cup rum
- 4 scoops vanilla ice cream

In flambé pan or skillet, melt butter. Add sugar, cinnamon, and banana liqueur; stir to mix. Bring to boil and simmer 2 minutes. Place bananas in sauce. Cook, stirring occasionally, till bananas are soft, about 4 minutes. Add rum; allow to heat slightly. Ignite. Serve over vanilla ice cream. Makes 4 servings.

Le Café

Poire Auberge de la Forêt
(Pears and Raspberries over Ice Cream)

- 1 cup water
- ¼ cup sugar
- 1 teaspoon vanilla
- 4 medium pears, peeled (with stems left on)
- 1 10-ounce package frozen red raspberries, thawed
- 2 tablespoons pear brandy or Cognac
- 4 scoops vanilla ice cream

In 10-inch skillet, combine water, sugar, and vanilla. Bring to boiling; add pears. Cover and simmer till tender, about 8 to 10 minutes, turning pears once. Remove pears; drain and set aside. Drain raspberries, reserving syrup. Add raspberry syrup to liquid in skillet. Boil hard to reduce to ⅓ cup (8 to 10 minutes). Remove from heat. Add pear brandy.

To serve, place a scoop of ice cream in each of 4 sherbet dishes. Make a slight depression in top of each with back of scoop. Place one pear upright in the depression of each serving of ice cream; spoon raspberries around base of pear. Drizzle with raspberry syrup. Serve immediately. Makes 4 servings.

THE
BISTRO
BEVERLY HILLS

Beverly Hills, California

Chocolate Soufflé

    5 egg yolks
  ½ cup sugar
  ¼ teaspoon vanilla
  ¾ cup all-purpose flour
    2 cups milk
    2 1-ounce squares unsweetened chocolate, melted and cooled
    8 egg whites
  ¼ cup sugar
      Powdered sugar
      Sweetened whipped cream

In small mixer bowl, beat egg yolks till thick; gradually beat in ½ cup sugar and vanilla. Gradually beat in flour. Add milk, beating till smooth. Transfer to saucepan. Cook and stir till thickened and bubbly, about 10 minutes. Remove from heat and stir in chocolate.

Beat egg whites till soft peaks form; gradually add ¼ cup sugar, beating till stiff peaks form. Stir a small amount of whites into yolk mixture to lighten. Fold into remaining egg whites.

Turn into 8 greased and sugared individual soufflé dishes. Bake in 350° oven for 30 to 35 minutes. Sprinkle with powdered sugar. Serve immediately with sweetened whipped cream. Makes 8 servings.

Crêpe of Soufflé Pigall's

    2 tablespoons butter or margarine
    2 tablespoons all-purpose flour
 1/3 cup milk
    3 beaten egg yolks
    3 egg whites
    1 teaspoon vanilla
 1/4 cup sugar
   12 6-inch dessert crêpes (page 124)
      . . .
    1 lemon
 1/3 cup water
    2 teaspoons cornstarch
    1 tablespoon water
 1/3 cup sugar
    1 tablespoon Kirsch (cherry brandy)

In saucepan, melt butter; blend in flour. Add milk; cook and stir till thickened and bubbly. Stir hot mixture into egg yolks; set aside. In small mixer bowl, beat egg whites and vanilla till soft peaks form. Gradually add the 1/4 cup sugar, beating to stiff peaks.

Fold egg yolk mixture into egg whites. Spoon egg mixture onto one side of crêpes, using about 1/3 cup for each. Roll up; place seam side down in lightly greased 13x9x2-inch baking dish. Bake, uncovered, in 400° oven for 10 minutes. Spoon sauce over crêpes to serve. Makes 6 servings.

Sauce: Remove yellow peel from lemon and cut into very thin slivers (about 1/4 cup). Squeeze juice from lemon (should have 3 tablespoons); set aside. Place lemon peel in small saucepan with the 1/3 cup water. Bring to boil; reduce heat and simmer, covered, 10 minutes. Combine cornstarch and the 1 tablespoon water; add to saucepan. Cook and stir till thickened and bubbly. Stir in the 1/3 cup sugar and the lemon juice; heat through. Add Kirsch.

Crêpe Soufflé

      4 egg whites
      1 cup sifted powdered sugar
      1 teaspoon finely shredded orange peel
    12 6-inch dessert crêpes*
    ⅓ cup granulated sugar
      2 teaspoons cornstarch
    ¼ teaspoon ground mace
      1 cup milk
    ½ cup light cream
      4 beaten egg yolks
    ½ teaspoon shredded orange peel
      2 tablespoons light rum

In small mixer bowl, beat egg whites to soft peaks. Gradually add powdered sugar, beating till stiff peaks form. Fold in the 1 teaspoon orange peel. Spoon meringue onto one side of each crêpe; roll up. Place in lightly greased 13x9x2-inch baking dish. Bake, uncovered, in 400° oven for 10 minutes.

Meanwhile, in medium saucepan, combine granulated sugar, cornstarch, and mace. Add milk, cream, egg yolks, and the ½ teaspoon orange peel. Cook and stir till thickened; don't boil. Remove from heat and stir in rum. Serve warm over crêpes. Makes 6 servings.

* **Dessert Crepes:** In bowl combine 1 cup all-purpose flour, 1½ cups milk, 2 eggs, 2 tablespoons sugar, 1 tablespoon cooking oil, and ⅛ teaspoon salt. Beat with rotary beater till blended. Heat a lightly greased 6-inch skillet. Remove from heat. Spoon in 2 tablespoons batter; lift and tilt skillet to spread batter. Return to heat; brown on one side. Invert pan over paper toweling; remove crêpe. Repeat, greasing skillet as needed. Makes 16 to 18 crêpes.

Soufflé Grand Marnier

- ½ cup milk
- 2 tablespoons granulated sugar
  Pinch of salt
- 2 tablespoons all-purpose flour
- 3 tablespoons cold milk
- ½ cup Grand Marnier liqueur
- 3 beaten egg yolks
- 2 teaspoons butter
- 4 stiffly beaten egg whites
  Powdered sugar

In saucepan, bring ½ cup milk, sugar, and salt to boil. Combine flour and 3 tablespoons cold milk; stir into hot milk mixture. Add liqueur. Then cook, stirring, for 2 to 3 minutes, or until thickened.

Remove from heat; add egg yolks and butter and at the last moment, add stiffly beaten egg whites. Mix quickly. Fill a 1-quart buttered and sugared soufflé dish. Smooth the surface of the soufflé. Bake in 375° to 400° oven for approximately 20 minutes or until golden in color. Sprinkle top with powdered sugar to glaze; serve immediately. Makes 2 servings.

RESTAURANT INDEX

San Francisco, *Fournou's Ovens.* (The Stanford Court), 905 California Street, (415-989-1910). Recipe for Praline Ice Cream Pie on page 113.

San Francisco, *India House Restaurant,* 350 Jackson Street, (415-392-0744). Recipe for Lamb Curry Khorma on page 51.

San Francisco, *Jack's,* 615 Sacramento Street, (415-421-7355). Recipe for Fried Cream with Rum on page 116.

San Francisco, *Kan's Chinese Restaurant,* 708 Grant Avenue, (415-982-2388). Recipe for Gah Lei Fon Ker Ngow Yuke on page 36.

San Francisco, *La Bourgogne,* 320 Mason Street, (415-362-7352). Recipe for Soufflé Grand Marnier on page 125.

San Francisco, *Le Club,* 1250 Jones Street, (415-771-5400). Recipe for Roast Duck with Orange and Cointreau on page 73.

San Francisco, *L'Etoile,* 1075 California Street, (415-771-1529). Recipe for L'Escalopine de Veau au Champagne on page 90.

San Francisco, *The Mandarin Restaurant,* Ghirardelli Square, 900 North Point, (415-673-8812). Recipe for Grilled and Steamed Chiao Tzu on page 58.

Santa Monica, *Madame Wu's Garden,* 2201 Wilshire Blvd., (213-828-5656). Recipe for Madame Wu's Shredded Chicken Salad on page 99.

Santa Monica, *Valentino Continental Cuisine,* 3115 Pico Blvd., (213-829-4313). Recipe for Rigatoni ai 4 Formaggi on page 9.

Sausalito, *Ondine,* 558 Bridgeway, (415-332-0791). Recipe for Scampi Ondine on page 85.

COLORADO

Colorado Springs, *Charles Court* (Broadmoor Hotel), (303-634-7711). Recipe for Potage Lady Curzon on page 25.

Denver, *The Quorum,* 233 E. Colfax Avenue, (303-861-8686). Recipe for Filet de Boeuf en Croûte on page 31.

CONNECTICUT

Ridgefield, *Stonehenge,* Danbury-Norwalk Road, (203-438-6511). Recipe for Stonehenge Apple Fritters on page 117.

FLORIDA

Dania, *Le Cordon Bleu,* 1201 N. Federal Hwy., (305-922-3519). Recipe for Belgian Chocolate Drink on page 11.

Fort Lauderdale, *The Down Under,* 3000 East Oakland Park Blvd., (305-563-4123). Recipe for Quiche Michele on page 60.

Fort Lauderdale, *Mai-Kai,* 3599 North Federal Highway, (305-563-3272). Recipe for Moonkist Coconut on page 13.

Fort Lauderdale, *Pier 66,* 2301 S.E. 17th Street Causeway, (305-524-0566). Recipe for Crab Fritters with Rebel Sauce on page 7.

Miami Beach, *Joe's Stone Crab Restaurant,* 227 Biscayne Street, (305-673-0365). Recipe for Shrimp Creole on page 83.

Palm Beach, *Petite Marmite Restaurant,* 315 Worth Ave., (305-655-0550). Recipe for Potatoes Amandine on page 107.

GEORGIA

Atlanta, *Houlihan's Old Place,* 3393 Peachtree Road N.E., (404-261-5323). Recipe for Crabacado Salad on page 97.

Savannah, *The Pirates' House,* 20 East Broad Street, (912-233-5757). Recipe for Grasshopper Pie on page 112.

ILLINOIS

Chicago, *The Bakery,* 2218 North Lincoln, (312-472-6942). Recipe for Roast Duckling with Cherry Glaze on page 66.

Chicago, *Biggs,* 1150 N. Dearborn Parkway, (312-787-0900). Recipe for Rack of Lamb with Cream Garlic Sauce on page 55.

Chicago, *Café de Paris,* 1260 N. Dearborn Parkway, (312-943-6080). Recipe for Pepper Steak, Café de Paris on page 29.

Chicago, *Cape Cod Room* (Drake Hotel), Lake Shore Drive and Upper Michigan Ave., (312-787-2200). Recipe for Pompano-Papillote à la Drake on page 43.

Chicago, *L'Epuisette,* 21 W. Goethe, (312-944-2288). Recipe for Stuffed Boneless Brook Trout on page 42.

Chicago, *Maxim's de Paris,* (Astor Hotel), 1300 N. Astor St., (312-943-1111). Recipe for Sole Albert on page 47.

Chicago, *Sea Gull,* 400 E. Randolph, (312-527-1390). Recipe for Stuffed Lobster Tails à la Sea Gull on page 78.

Wheeling, *Le Francais,* 269 S. Milwaukee Ave.,
(312-541-7470). Recipe for Coquilles St.
Jacques Petits Legumes on page 87.

INDIANA

Fort Wayne, *Cafe Johnell,* 2529 South Calhoun
St., (219-456-1939). Recipe for Truite Soufflé
on page 39.

LOUISIANA

Gretna, *Le Ruth's,* 636 Franklin St.,
(504-362-4914). Recipe for Lump Crab Meat
and Crayfish Cardinal on page 80.

New Orleans, *Brennan's,* 417 Royal St.,
(504-525-9711). Recipe for Bananas Foster
on page 120.

New Orleans, *Masson's Restaurant Francais,*
7200 Pontchartrain Blvd., (504-283-2525).
Recipe for Oysters Beach House on page 3.

New Orleans, *Pontchartrain Hotel,* (Caribbean
Room), 2031 St. Charles Ave., (504-524-0581).
Recipe for Crêpe Soufflé on page 124.

MARYLAND

Baltimore, *Chesapeake,* 1701 North Charles St.,
(301-837-7711). Recipe for Teriyaki Sauce
Chesapeake on page 27.

Baltimore, *Danny's,* 1201 N. Charles St.,
(301-539-1393). Recipe for Steak Diane,
Flambé on page 33.

Baltimore, *Gordon's,* Orleans St. at Patterson
Park Ave., (301-732-2040). Recipe for
Oyster Chowder on page 24.

MASSACHUSETTS

Boston, *Cafe Budapest,* 90 Exeter St.,
(617-734-3388). Recipe for Mushrooms Stuffed
with Breast of Turkey on page 74.

Boston, *Locke-Ober,* 3-4 Winter Place,
(617-542-1340). Recipe for Baked Lobster
Savannah on page 79.

MICHIGAN

Dearborn, *Kyoto Japanese Steak House,*
18601 Hubbard Drive, (313-593-3200). Recipe
for Dipping Sauces on page 59.

Detroit, *Joe Muer's,* 2000 Gratiot Ave.,
(313-962-1088). Recipe for Flounder Stuffed
with Deviled Crab on page 48.

Detroit, *London Chop House,* 155 West
Congress, (313-962-1087). Recipe for
Watercress Soup on page 16.

Detroit, *Pontchartrain Wine Cellars,* 234 W. Larned, (313-963-1785). Recipe for Blanquette de Veau on page 91.

Troy, *Charley's Crab,* 5498 Crooks Road, (313-879-2060). Recipe for Baked Stuffed Lobster Larry on page 77.

MINNESOTA

Bloomington, *Le Café* (L'hotel Sofitel), I-494 and Highway 100, (612-835-1900). Recipe for Poire Auberge de la Forêt on page 120.

Minneapolis, *Charlie's Cafe Exceptionale,* 701 Fourth Ave. S., (612-335-8851). Recipe for Braised Viennese Pork Roast on page 57.

St. Paul, *The Blue Horse,* 1355 University Ave., (612-645-8101). Recipe for Roast Filet of Beef-Pérgourdine on page 32.

MISSOURI

St. Louis, *Tony's,* 826 N. Broadway, (314-231-7007). Recipe for Zabaglione on page 119.

NEBRASKA

Omaha, *The French Cafe,* 1017 Howard St., (402-341-3547). Recipe for Gâteau Moelleux d' Asperges on page 105.

NEVADA

Las Vegas, *Bacchanal Restaurant* (Caesars Palace), 3570 Las Vegas Blvd., (702-731-7338). Recipe for Steak Flambé Moutarde on page 28.

NEW MEXICO

Santa Fe, *The Pink Adobe,* 406 Old Santa Fe Trail, (505-983-9976). Recipe for Poulet Marengo Pink Adobe on page 63.

NEW YORK

Brooklyn, *Gage and Tollner,* 372 Fulton Street, (212-875-5181). Recipe for Bay Scallops Newburg on page 81.

Elmira Heights, *Pierce's 1894 Restaurant,* 228 Oakwood Ave., (607-734-2022). Recipe for Pork Medallions à la Lida Lee on page 61.

Hillsdale, *L'Hostellerie Bressane,* Routes 22 and 23 (518-325-3412). Recipes for Crème de Pois a L'Oseille on page 17.

Hillsdale, *Swiss Hütte,* Route 23, (518-325-3333). Recipe for Côte de Veau Normande on page 95.

New York City, *Antolotti's,* 337 East 49th St., (212-688-6767). Recipe for Shrimp Antolotti on page 84.

New York City, *The Four Seasons,* 99 East 52nd St., (212-754-9494). Recipe for Baked Tartar of Red Snapper and Bay Scallops on page 41.

New York City, *Gaylord (India) Restaurant,* 50 East 58th St., (212-759-1710). Recipe for Chhole Masala on page 108.

New York City, *La Caravelle,* 33 West 55th St., (212-586-4252). Recipe for Crème Nouvelle France on page 20.

New York City, *Le Manoir,* 120 East 56th St., (212-753-1447). Recipe for Rouget Grillé Beurre Nantaise on page 49.

New York City, *Lutèce,* 249 East 50th St., (212-752-2225). Recipe for Coq Sauté au Riesling d' Alsace on page 64.

New York City, *Ristorante Toscana,* 246 East 54th St., (212-371-8144). Recipe for Paglia e Fieno on page 9.

New York City, *The Russian Tea Room,* 150 W. 57th St., (212-265-0947). Recipe for Cotelette à la Kiev on page 65.

New York City, *Shun Lee Dynasty,* 900 Second Ave., (212-755-3900). Recipe for Hunan Beef on page 37.

New York City, *The "21" Club,* 21 West 52nd St., (212-582-7200). Recipe for Cold Salmon "21" with Pressed Cucumbers and Sauce Verte on page 5.

New York City, *Windows on the World,* 107th Floor, One World Trade Center, (212-938-1111). Recipe for Tintoretto on page 13.

OHIO
Cincinnati, *Maisonette,* 114 East Sixth St., (513-721-2260). Recipe for Epinards au Beurre ou à la Crème on page 106.

Cincinnati, *Pigall's,* 127 West 4th St., (513-721-1245). Recipe for Crêpe of Soufflé Pigall's on page 123.

OREGON
Portland, *L'Omelette,* 815 S.W. Alder, (503-248-9661). Recipe for Ballotines de Volaille on page 69.

PENNSYLVANIA
East Petersburg, *Haydn Zug's,* (717-569-5746). Recipe for Cheesey Chowder on page 19.

Lancaster, *The Lemon Tree,* 1766 Columbia Ave., (717-394-0441). Recipe for Veau à la Crème aux Chataigne on page 93.

Philadelphia, *Les Amis,* 1920 Chestnut St., (215-567-0855). Recipe for Trout Talloires on page 40.

Philadelphia, *Old Original Bookbinder's,* 125 Walnut St., (215-925-7027). Recipe for Old Original Bookbinder's Snapper Soup on page 21.

Pottstown, *Coventry Forge Inn,* (215-469-6222). Recipe for Crabe Wallis on page 80.

Wrightsville, *Accomac Inn,* (717-252-1521). Recipe for Carré d'Agneau en Croûte on page 52.

SOUTH CAROLINA

Charleston, *Perdita's,* 10 Exchange St., (803-577-4364). Recipe for St. Honoré Pie on page 111.

TEXAS

Austin, *Green Pastures,* 811 W. Live Oak, (512-444-4747). Recipe for Milk Punch on page 11.

Dallas, *La Vieille Varsovie,* 2610 Maple Ave., (214-528-0032). Recipe for Old Warsaw Salad on page 98.

Houston, *Bismarck,* 719 Franklin, (713-227-4168). Recipe for Crêpe St. Jacques on page 1.

San Antonio, *La Louisiane,* 2632 Broadway, (512-225-7984). Recipe for deGaulle or Cresson Salad Dressing on page 102.

VERMONT

Manchester, *Toll Gate Lodge,* Route 11 and Route 30, (802-362-1779). Recipe for Supreme of Capon Smitane on page 71.

WASHINGTON

Seattle, *Ray's Boat House,* 6049 Seaview N.W., (206-789-3770). Recipe for Marinated Lamb on page 53.

WEST VIRGINIA

White Sulphur Springs, *The Greenbrier,* (304-536-1110). Recipe for Soufflé de Sole Anglaise on page 46.

WISCONSIN

Milwaukee, *Karl Ratzsch's,* 320 East Mason St., (414-276-2720). Recipe for Walnut Nut Roll on page 103.

RECIPE INDEX

A

B

C

D

E

F

G

H

L

M

O

P

Q

R

S

T

V

W

Z

Brennan's

Louisiane

The Russian T

Windsor

THE Down Under
FOOD & SPIRITS

Four
ove

La Bourgo

Pigall's

puisette

THE SAR
DINING·COCKTAIL
701 WAVE STREET
FACTO

RISTORANTE
Toscana

Le Café

madame wu

e Johnell